Remarkable Guidance

REMARKABLE GUIDANCE

*A true story of a life lovingly directed
by God and guardian angels*

SHELLY MORROW WHITENBURG

TATE PUBLISHING
AND ENTERPRISES, LLC

Published by Tate Publishing & Enterprises, LLC
127 E. Trade Center Terrace | Mustang, Oklahoma 73064 USA
1.888.361.9473 | www.tatepublishing.com

Tate Publishing is committed to excellence in the publishing industry. The company reflects the philosophy established by the founders, based on Psalm 68:11,
"The Lord gave the word and great was the company of those who published it."

Book design copyright © 2014 by Tate Publishing, LLC. All rights reserved.
Cover design by Nikolai Purpura
Interior design by Caypeeline Casas

Published in the United States of America

ISBN: 978-1-63185-406-4
Religion / Christian Life / Inspirational
14.06.11

*This book is dedicated with all the
love that I have in my heart,
first and foremost to God,
to my guardian angels,
and to my husband, Wade.*

SCRIPTURES

For He shall give His angels charge over thee,
to keep thee in all thy ways.

Psalm 91:11 (KJV)

To every thing there is a season, and a time to
every purpose under the heaven.

Ecclesiastes 3 (KJV)

Don't worry about anything; instead pray about
everything. Tell God what you need, and thank
Him for all He has done.

Philippians 4:6 (NLT)

For the wages of sin is death, but the gift of
God is eternal life.

Romans 6:23 (NIV)

CONTENTS

REMARKABLE STORIES

FOREWORD

I have been given a gift, and it is a gift of knowledge of God and guardian angels. This gift has come to me after many years of my own soul-searching, and it is something that I know in my heart, is knowledge that is supposed to be shared.

Perhaps this gift has come to me because for the last thirty plus years, I have been a seeker and have been on my own spiritual quest, determined to rise above challenges in my world. Perhaps it is because I am very open-minded and that I am accepting to the probability that there is so much more to life than can be seen. Perhaps it is because I have an unwavering belief in God and in Jesus and in my own guardian angels. (Perhaps: adv: possibly but not certainly, the *Merriam-Webster Dictionary*.)

The thing that I know for certain is that the interesting experiences that led to the unveiling of this gift are real, and they are experiences that I have kept to myself and a handful of people for many years. But through a series of events and as I meet people who have incredible stories of their own, which I tell in this book, it gives me courage to tell mine.

I don't know why I have had so many unique experiences. I don't know why I am being prompted to talk about guardian angels. I do not know for certain what this is all about, but God knows, and I have to trust in that alone.

This is my story about how a little rhyme that just came to me in 1997 became a children's book. It is about how I learned to conquer the challenges in my own life and how I saw positive results in my life, as well as those in my inner circle, when I did. It is about how I learned to communicate with God and my guardian angels and how I built a relationship that empowered me to keep believing and to have such faith in God, that I truly trust the process of life, no matter how things appear to be.

Writing this book is a dream of mine, and it has been in my heart to do this for years. What I find quite remarkable is how I even got to this place where I am fulfilling my heart's desire. I am being guided to write this book, which is one of many interesting experiences that I have had so far, but I will mainly focus on the ones that are pertinent to my story.

And it is a story that I am supposed to tell.

REMARKABLE ANGELS

Confirmation that the help is right there beside us all.

For He shall give His angels charge over thee,
to keep thee in all thy ways.

Psalm 91:11

ME...IT'S WHO I AM

"Just write, it will all come together" are the words that frequently come to my mind. "Just write" are the reoccurring thoughts. I am being guided to write my story, and I have a tendency to allow myself to be stifled, waiting for the perfect scenario before I start something. But the perfect scenario usually doesn't transpire, and it just leads me to procrastinate even longer, which I also have a tendency to do.

So I am determined to stay on top of that part of me that can get distracted by the things on my daily list of things to do as my job as a stay-at-home mom and now a children's book author. I am making myself stay focused on the priorities of which I have put writing *Remarkable Guidance*, along with making sure that the bills are paid, appointments are kept, and that my family has food to eat and clean clothes to wear. I can let the dust build up and things temporarily fall apart around the home for a little while longer because I know in my heart that this is what I am supposed be doing as of right now. This is a purpose that I have to fulfill.

I have learned to pay attention to repetitive thoughts that come to me because I have found that many times there is a reason behind these thoughts, and when I trust what comes to me, it usually puts me on the right path. But all of that has to follow what I feel is right in my heart because if it is genuinely good, it is more in alignment with God. And when things are aligned with God, everything falls into perfect balance, and I like it when life balances out. I feel very content, satisfied, and happy.

This place where I am today, where I live more through my heart than through my head, has come after thirty plus years of conducting my own soul-searching and self-discovery. I have taken a path where I now feel as if I have unlocked some of the mysteries of life, and it is a path that has led me to having a steadfast relationship with God.

My personal path in life started off with me being taught to believe in God and in the wonderful teachings of Jesus Christ as many kids in America are taught. But knowing God comes through living life whereas having a relationship with God, for me, has come through learning how to communicate on more of a consistent basis and that has come through having a lot of interesting and challenging experiences.

I kind of did things backwards in life than what was represented by the typical American families of the 1960s in that I didn't start off going to church every Sunday to learn of God. That happened a few times when I was young, but divorce interrupted the flow of my American family, so we never really followed the typical route. My route was a bit more jagged and bumpy along the way, but I now sit in a church that teaches scripture in a comfortable way that resonates to the core of my soul because I truly get it. It makes sense to me because I have lived it.

Most of the spiritual awareness in my life has come through observing my mom, whose strength persevered during very trying times in her life. Though she grew up in an impoverished situation and then later in a Baptist orphanage in the 1940s and '50s, resulting in having no family that she could count on, I never saw or heard her complain or wallow in her past. She did her very best to make sure that her kids had a much better start to life than she did. I learned by watching Mom that when you stumble along the way, you pick yourself right back up and move yourself forward with grace and dignity. And if you need to cave, do so—but only for a little while—and never, never give in!

The only thing that Mom truly had to lean on in life was her unwavering faith in God, and it got her through some pretty rough times and later on to much smoother roads. This determination to not be dependent on any person or anything in life but God had a deep impact on me.

I have always been more of an observer than a communicator and have been comfortable learning by paying attention to the world around me. My parents had three children come into this world in a span of two years, so as a child, I learned what worked and what didn't work by paying attention to my younger sister and brother who tested the rules and boundaries a lot! I was very sensitive, and all that Mom would have to do was give me a stern look of disapproval, enough so that I would get that I needed to make some adjustments. And I would because I knew that I didn't like the outcome based on what I had learned through my eyes, through my ears, and through my gut. If I felt a hint of uneasiness, it usually meant that the end result was not good.

Paying attention to the feeling is something that I would later realize is a pretty good gauge to staying on the right track.

Our parent's marriage was rocky and was teetering on the edge of divorce, which I was oblivious to, so Mom had been equipping herself with a teacher's degree at the local university for that just-in-case and, most likely, probable scenario. That scenario started to play out when I was almost ten years old, right after our baby sister was born. Our parents divorced, and by the time I completed fifth grade, we uprooted and moved to a nearby town where Mom found a teaching position at an elementary school.

Life abruptly changed from carefree days of just being a kid who absolutely loved spending time outdoors, traipsing around the woods, creek beds, and cow pastures with my brother and sister, or raking up pine needles to form the outlines of walls and doors for my make-believe house underneath the tall, flexible pine trees. It seemed as though I was always outside riding bikes, climbing trees, fishing for crawdaddies, or just living in my own imaginary, exploratory world that seemed to have limitless boundaries.

The days of having a stay-at-home mom were over, and I immediately fell into the responsibility role of helping to care for our little sister while feeling the stress of a working parent who was trying to juggle it all. Money was limited, so Mom held three jobs at times to help make ends meet. Dad was sporadically in the picture, which was sometimes fun, but he was caught in his own tangled web of challenges, so wasn't reliable. I started learning that there are a lot of challenges in life and that life is not always comfortable and that the world is filled with many limiting factors. Boundaries were now very apparent to me, and it did not feel good.

Aside from being the new kid on the block, I was a skinny girl with terribly crooked teeth and hair that was starting to get completely unmanageable. All of this, plus the feeling of being like a fish out of water only accentuated the insecurities that I felt when I was outside the perimeters of my comfort zone, which was my family and a few close friends who now lived a couple of small towns away.

I was now officially in junior high school, so my insecurities led me to being picked on, mainly by one particular girl who perhaps viewed me as being weak. Perhaps I was weak, but I started to become stronger after Mom somehow made it work out for me to get my teeth straightened by the next-door neighbor who was just starting his own orthodontic practice. It took a couple of years, but once the braces came off, it was like sticking the wilted flower that I was into a vase of water. I felt refreshed and renewed and I began to feel more comfortable with who I was becoming.

I started earning a little money by babysitting when I was twelve, and I say a little money because seventy-five cents an hour was the going rate and that was not on a per child basis as it sometimes is today. It was hard work for little pay, but it was rewarding at times because I remember feeling so helpful when Mom needed to borrow money just to get by. It was empowering and it made me want to strive for a better future, so I set my sights on going to college. This was really not an option in my mind because the kids in school were focused on continuing their education and my parents had college degrees as well. It was always something that I knew I would do.

I worked during my high school years and saved a little more money to add to the babysitting income that I had been collecting and then took out a student loan to put myself through college. I was ready to be free for a while from the responsibilities of my home life and was looking forward to new experiences, as I had missed out on a few milestones like going to home-coming games or to prom. By this time in my life, I was more sure of myself and was definitely ready to get involved in campus life. I joined a sorority, became a little sister to a fraternity, and I started dating Wade, whom I would later marry.

Those four years in college was a time for me to truly spread my wings for a while, and those were some of the best years of my life. It was such a great training ground to start to really discover who I am—What are my strengths and weaknesses? What am I passionate

about? What drives me? What stifles me? What brings
me joy?

I have spent years getting to know me, and I am still
on this amazing discovery tour of who I am, and if I
have learned anything noteworthy, it would be this—I
know, without a hint of doubt, that there is such assistance with life that comes through communicating
what is on my mind and what is in my heart.

GUARDIAN ANGELS

Talking is how I got to this place where I am here now, writing this book, and how I became an author of a children's book about knowing that guardian angels are here as assistants to God. I just started talking through my written word, through my spoken word, and through my thinking word.

I started doing this on my own when I was in seventh grade. I remember this because I lived in eleven different houses by the time I graduated from high school, so I can remember what grade I was in by what house I lived in at that particular time in my life. This has always come in handy when remembering when a certain song came out or when a show was popular on TV or when certain products were introduced to the market. Experience and ages are easy for me to peg in my personal memory bank, especially in my early years.

Seventh grade must have been the year that I started becoming more aware of challenges, not just in my own world, but around the globe. The year was 1973, and something that I must have seen on the news made me afraid of our country going into war. I just remember being very concerned about war in general, so my twelve-year-old self took it upon myself to start saying prayers when I went to bed. I found that saying prayers comforted me and helped me to sleep well at night.

I would always start off with a simple children's prayer or the Lord's Prayer. Then I would say a short prayer about being thankful for that particular day, and I would end it with a more specific prayer. The last prayer was always more about praying for what I knew was going on the following day, such as asking for help with taking a test that was being administered or to help me make good choices in general. But what seemed most important to me was asking for me and my family to be kept safe and for America to be kept safe too. The thought of war terrified me.

For more than twenty-five years, I never ceased saying three prayers every night before I went to sleep. I have no idea why I felt like I needed to say three prayers, but in retrospect, I kept doing it because everything that I prayed about worked. So I kept at it. I knew in my heart that it was my saving grace. It didn't mean that I wouldn't have tough times to contend with, because I did and at times still do, but it has always helped me to get through those times.

So, I continued to talk and pray, and as time has gone by and as I have maneuvered through life with its incredible ups and its ever so challenging downs, I have gotten better and better at it. I no longer say three prayers at night, though I start my day and end my day with prayers. I am now in a continuous mode of communicating through my thoughts and my words, and I do this because life falls into place, many times so perfectly that there is no way my human self could have conjured up a better picture or scenario. Everything flows—and I mean everything!

I have, for many years now, believed that there is so much more to life than can be seen. I know that I have a lot of help, and sometimes, the help seems to be right there because the answer or assistance is immediate. I know that my concerns, my requests, and my prayers to God are being attended to, deciphered, and fulfilled in some way or another. I know this because I am now more consciously aware of the answers to my communication, resulting in many experiences that confirm to me that I am being heard and listened to and assisted in ways that can only be described as a "God thing." It is all sometimes so seemingly perfect!

I believe that God gave us guardian angels as escorts on this life journey that we each take on, and I believe that they are with us from the beginning of the start point on one's individualized and personal path of life until the path reaches its finishing point. I believe that no matter how long or short or crooked or rocky the personal paths of life are, that guardian angels are there doing their "angel thing": sheltering, guiding, assisting, supporting, prodding, comforting, etc., with such a love and a willingness to be even more helpful when recognized and called into action, especially when the assignment is honorable and has value and is helpful to life.

As a child, I had seen an angel, though had completely forgotten about it until I was home one weekend from college. It was a beautiful September day, and

Mom and I were sitting outside catching up on life, and we must have gotten to a place where we were talking about angels. My mom has always been my spiritual teacher and advisor, and we have had many wonderful and enlightening conversations throughout the years. At one point during our conversation, she says to me, "I remember when you were little and you kept talking about seeing an angel."

The moment that Mom voiced those few words to me, the memory of it rushed back to me as if it had happened the day before! It was as if a door that had been shut for seventeen years had now been unlocked and opened, and the vision and the feeling came whooshing out for me to examine. It was an amazing feeling and recollection of a memory stored away long ago in the archives of my brain, that was destined to be retrieved at some point in time, and this was that point in time.

I must have been three or four years old, but I remember that I had been sleeping, and that I was in that in-between sleep state where I was aware of outside noises, yet I was still in a state of slumber. This in-between sleep state is where I have had lots of interesting experiences.

My parents must have had company over that evening because I recall hearing adults conversing and laughing in another room outside of my bedroom. I stirred and briefly opened my eyes and saw a life-sized, fully robed, winged angel standing to my left near the foot of my bed. The angel was standing like a silent sentinel, with his head bowed as if in a resting mode. I remember feeling comforted and not concerned in the least, and went back to la-la land to finish my sleep.

Well, apparently, I talked a lot about it at the time, which was something not really encouraged back in the 1960s, so subsequently, I forgot about it and put it into a storage box, tucked it away, and marked it as worthy of being retrieved on a future date in time.

Thirty plus years have gone by since I collected that storage box, so I have been consciously aware of their help now for a long time. During the last seventeen years, I have had many remarkable experiences that confirm for me that I have the help right there beside me. I am very aware that even though I may be physically alone, I never am truly alone, and I take great comfort in that realization.

I cannot imagine living in this world without their glorious assistance.

THE RHYME

My communication with God and my guardian angels intensified when I became a mom in 1991. Having a child that was completely dependent on me brought forth so many fears along with an unfathomable amount of joy, so I found myself asking God and my guardian angels for their protection, for their peace, for their wisdom, and for things such as helping me to find the time to be able to take a short nap or get some things accomplished around the house. I needed their assistance because I am extremely independent in nature and I was not good at asking others for help.

So as Brooke became a full-blown and very adventurous toddler at the ripe age of nine months, and soon after, when friends became a part of her world, I seemed to always be saying "Angels keep her safe," "Angels keep them safe," as she and/or her friends ran around joyously engaged in play. It seemed as though I was always asking them for their protection because my human body and mind are so limited in their capabilities. I, of myself, can only do so much.

When I made the decision to be a stay-at-home mom, it was one of the best and toughest decisions that

I have ever had to make. By the time Brooke was born, I had been working for six years in the human resources department of a large natural gas pipeline company. My job was to interview and hire people for secretarial and clerical positions, and I was also responsible for the hiring of temporary personnel as well. It was great fun, and I had such an appreciation for my job, for the team that I worked with, and for the company as well.

I absolutely loved my job to the point where I honestly thought that I would be able to juggle the act of working and being a mom like so many amazing women do. I know that I would have been able to do so, but my heart was telling me otherwise.

Meanwhile, my maternity leave was ticking away and I had not made the time to look around for a means of a substitute. Wade, who sensed that he was maneuvering ever so carefully on very thin ice, cautiously asked me if I was planning on going back to work. I bawled at the thought of me not being there for Brooke, but I knew that I had to make a definite decision, so I visited one wonderful lady who took care of kids in her home.

I could tell that the children that she cared for loved her, and at one point, she had to excuse herself to put one of the children down for a nap. The lady came back apologizing, saying that the little girl had been at her home since six that morning. She said that if she didn't make sure that she took her nap, the little girl would be out by seven, which was an hour after she would have been picked up following a long day of work.

That sealed it for me, and I knew immediately that I was supposed to stay home and that somehow God would help it work out financially for us to do so. After almost letting my six weeks of maternity leave expire, I finally gave up my beloved job and started a whole new way of living. It was tough, but it felt right.

Wade's job required him to travel extensively, so the bulk of the responsibility of raising Brooke and staying on top of domestic responsibilities and the managing of our lives fell primarily on my shoulders. I took care of most everything so that our lives on the weekends would be as stress-free as possible. Spending time together as a family was extremely important to me, and I wanted Brooke to feel and know the importance of the bond of a stable, happy family.

I found great joy in being at home with Brooke, yet at times, I felt stifled and limited. I did have interactions with other moms and their children, which helped tremendously, but there was this big part of me that wanted to have a job, yet there was this even bigger part of me that wanted to be there for my child. I needed something else, but was not sure what that was.

The domestic tasks of managing a home can get pretty repetitive and mundane, so I found myself bored at times. There were many times when I thought that there had to be something better to do with my time than always cleaning and organizing our home, sorting through paperwork, and trying to figure out what to feed people three times a day. I sometimes felt as though I was caught in a monotonous spin cycle of things that needed to be done!

My salary went by the wayside and was no longer a part of our income, so I did what I could do to lesson the financial responsibility on Wade. I became a recycler and a coupon clipper and a bargain hunter. I even tried running a couple of businesses out of our home, but never to the point where I was making any money, so those ventures didn't last long. I just wound up having inventory to add to my already, at times, cluttered home.

I found that I wasn't necessarily good at setting aside a certain amount of time for business every day. Each day was a different story and spontaneous outings to the park or to a playmate's house took precedence. As long as my child was happy, I was happy, so I resigned myself from carrying the weight of having a job outside of the home and committed myself to trying to be the best wife and mom that I could be. I wanted to try to create a pleasant home environment for us all. It was my job, even though it didn't bring in any noticeable income, and it was a job that I completely took to heart.

It was August of 1997 when the rhyme just came to me. By this time, Wade and I had been married for eleven years and Brooke was now six years old. Brooke had just started first grade and I was looking forward to having some time to explore possibilities of doing something constructive with my extra time. I was ready to volunteer or perhaps find a part-time job. I was ready for something that challenged my brain in a new and fulfilling way.

On this particular day, while Brooke was enjoying her first couple of days at school, I was busy vacuuming our home and I realized that I had a rhyme swirling around in my head. I stopped what I was doing, grabbed a pen and paper, and jotted it down word for word.

Angels are God's helpers.
They brighten our every day.
They guide and protect us at home,
work, and play.
They are with us when we are happy and
when we are sad
And even when we are very, very mad!
Angels are patient, kind, and full of love.
They are here to assist us from way up above.
They do not judge, criticize, nor condemn.
They want us to see the good in all men.
Angels are not easy to see or to hear
But they are always right with us,
lending an ear.
So take comfort in knowing that things are
always fine
Even if things seem to be out of line.
Call upon your angels to help you see
Just how wonderful things in life can be!

I gave the rhyme two titles: "In the Presence of Angels" or "Our Guardian Angels." I typed it up and then put it to the side. I thought that it was pretty neat how that little rhyme just came through me. I certainly believed in guardian angels. I just did not know at the time how incredible this experience would wind up being.

Unbeknownst to me, this was just the remarkable beginning of a divine gift that was being handed to me.

EXTRAORDINARY SIGNS

I have always been so curious about the diverse nature of people and life, and in the early years of my spiritual quest, my curiosity led me to exploring some of the mysteries of life; things that couldn't necessarily be explained in textbooks. I was particularly drawn to stories of people's personal accounts of out of the ordinary experiences, which led me to have a very open-minded view of people and of the world in general. There are a lot of interesting stories out there, so there is not much that really surprises me. I was never taught to not believe in strange occurrences or to shy away or shun people who might think outside of the box. This allowed me the freedom to come to my own conclusions, and this is what helped me to be ready for my own interesting experiences.

Seeing an angel as a child was my out of the ordinary experience by the time the rhyme was planted in my head. I say planted because I did not consciously decide to sit down one day to compose a rhyme about guardian angels. The rhyme was like a seed being gently placed into my brain and kept there until I could give it a permanent form. Then it was fertilized with two extraordinary signs that would help it to one day grow into a sweet children's book. I was the soil for the seed, and later, I would be the gardener. I was just unaware of what my future occupation would entail.

The first extraordinary sign happened within a week of the planting process. Wade was on a business trip, so it was just me and Brooke at home. On this particular morning, Brooke was watching a favorite morning show before she went to school. At one point, I passed in front of a bookcase that stood next to the couch that she was sitting on to bring her something to drink, and then I retreated back to the kitchen to prepare breakfast and pack her lunch kit for school.

The bottom two rows of this bookcase perfectly hold a set of Britannica Great Books of the Western World, which my parents had purchased in the early 1960s. The books have always been tightly wedged together and are really more for show than for use as their spines are brittle. They look nice sitting on the shelves, and they give me less surface area to dust, which is important for a mom who is already stretched with enough things on her list to take care of. I carried on with the morning business of getting Brooke ready and off to school.

After I got back home from walking to school that beautiful morning with my girl, I decided to clean up the morning mess left in the kitchen as well as tidy things up before I got on with my day. I finished up my kitchen duties and then I went into the living room to gather and straighten up whatever might be out of place. I was about to pass in front of the bookcase when I noticed that two books were now haphazardly lying on the floor. Somehow, the books had been pulled out of their place and had toppled onto the floor from the upper of the two shelves. This all took place in a matter of forty-five minutes.

Discovering the books on the floor was not a cause for alarm for me because I had read enough fascinating stories throughout the years that assured me that this could be a sign, which I found to be so exciting! I thought that maybe there was a message that I might read on one of the pages that was exposed when the books fell onto the floor, so I sat on the couch and scoured the pages, yet didn't find anything that I could interpret as a message for me. I was perplexed as to what this experience might mean and thought that I might not ever really know, so I chalked it up as a very neat, out of the ordinary experience, and eagerly got on with the tasks of the day. I smiled and thought "Wow, that was fun," and I approached the rest of that week with a bounce in my step.

Life was beginning to become more fun for me because I was finally starting to have other things to focus on other than being a wife, a mom, and a "manager of domestic affairs." I started volunteering at Brooke's school, I got involved with her Brownie troop, and I took care of making sure that she was present and ready at sports practices and games. I was beginning to realize that I function much more efficiently when I have commitments that I need to be prepared for. I work much better under pressure.

I was under a little pressure two weeks after the first extraordinary sign occurred. I had been out running errands that day and came home from grocery shopping with only a few minutes to spare before I had to meet Brooke after the school day to walk her home. I unloaded my SUV and set the bags of groceries on the floor and on top of the kitchen counters. I hurriedly put the dairy products in the refrigerator and the frozen items in the freezer, and I bolted out the door to quickly get to the school.

Anytime that I entered our kitchen, which happened several times a day, I always noticed the wooden angel that hung on the wall behind the stove cook top. Raffia, tied in the shape of a bow, was attached to the wire that held the angel. It was hard to miss seeing her, and it always made me smile when I did.

We arrived home after our leisurely fifteen minute walk from the school and while Brooke ventured upstairs to her room, I went into the kitchen to put the rest of the groceries away. Immediately, I noticed that the wooden angel wasn't hanging above the stove cook top anymore. The angel was now resting and perfectly centered on the edge of the counter to the left of the stove, with the raffia draped neatly in front of the cabinet drawer.

Overwhelmed and beside myself with the most incredible feeling of wonder and excitement, I said to God, "What is happening? This is crazy! What are you trying to tell me?" Another extraordinary sign had taken place during a short period of time! It was truly beyond comprehension. A message was perhaps being delivered to me, and it was up to me to interpret the signs effectively. There had to be a reason behind this form of communication, but I honestly did not know what to think. I just found it fun, and I chalked it up as another very neat experience. Now I had an even bigger bounce in my step!

I kept those stories to myself and just a few friends and family for a long time. The only thing that I could tie those experiences to was the rhyme that came to me. The first experience had to do with books, with the next experience having to do with angels. Books…angels… angel book? My thought was that I was supposed to turn the rhyme into a book. It was just a thought because I honestly did not know what this was all about. It was pretty unbelievable.

Well, unbelievable things sometimes have a way of becoming believable because fourteen more years would go by before that one would manifest. And remarkably so, it did that very thing.

MORE GUARDIAN ANGELS

1999 was the year that our family of three became a family of four. That February, we were blessed with a son, whom we named Luke. Brooke had just turned eight years old, so she proudly assumed the responsibility of being the best big sister a brother could ask for or a parent could wish for. We were blessed beyond reason.

Life was rewarding and stressful and exhausting at times, but because of this, I became even better at relying on God and my guardian angels for help. I was still learning how to lean on something much grander than my own self on a more consistent basis because my puny human self was slowly learning that it could only make things work for just so long. I still had some stubborn tendencies and control issues and just downright laziness that superseded at times.

Before Luke was born, I was pretty good at finding a moment to write my thoughts and feelings down in a spiral notebook that I kept in a bedside drawer. That was starting to dwindle some, mainly because of time constraints, so I started speaking more about what was on my mind. Some days, I was good about making the time to talk and to pray, and other days, I was too busy or too exhausted to do so. But what I found was when I did take the time to just talk about what was coming up for that day or for that week for me and my family and when I asked for things to flow well with everything going on, things did fall into its perfect place and it was good. And sometimes, it was even better than good. Sometimes, it was great!

Three years had now gone by since the unexplained happenings of 1997. Nothing really unusual had occurred since then. Those very interesting experiences were filed away in my personal memory bank, sometimes being retrieved to share with another open-minded person who wouldn't think that I was strange because they had their own curious stories to share as well. Thankfully, I was blessed with family and a few friends who, at the least, seemed to accept my sometimes peculiar ways of thinking.

I occasionally wondered if I might have another extraordinary story one day to file in that folder marked Strange and Mysterious Occurrences. I thought that it would be pretty neat if something interesting did happen, but what I failed to contemplate was that my next unusual experience might come through my children. After all, things don't necessarily happen the way a person might expect. "A watched pot never boils."

I was usually the one who put the kids to bed because Wade's travels required him to be gone during most weeks, and kids get very used to certain routines, so I was expected by my kids to handle the bulk of their bedtime routine. The routine that Luke was used to having was for us to sit together in the gliding rocking chair, read a story or two, and then I would rock him for a while before putting him into his crib for the night.

One evening, when Luke was about eighteen months old, he was just starting to nod off and I was about to put him in his crib, when all of a sudden, his eyes popped open and he became fixated at something on the wall. There was a polka-dotted dinosaur holding balloons in his mouth that hung on the wall above his crib, but he wasn't looking at the dinosaur. He was focused on the blank wall to the right of the dinosaur.

Immense joy filled Luke's face and he started smiling and waving his left hand at the blank wall. He continued to wave while his gaze and giant smile slowly followed whatever he was seeing to the center of the room. His gaze remained there just for a few seconds, then he slowly followed that which was invisible to me back to the same point on the blank wall. Luke sweetly says, "Night night," and then closes his eyes and goes immediately to sleep.

I was speechless and in complete awe with what I had just witnessed! I cannot explain the insurmountable joy that I felt with what I had just experienced through the eyes of my child. I had never even heard or read of a story like this. This experience filled my heart with such happiness and peace because that which was hidden from view for me, obviously had such love for Luke. Perhaps he saw his guardian angel.

As crazy as this may sound, the story does not stop here. Brooke and Luke's bedrooms were side by side at that time. Brooke's bed was positioned to where she could see the upstairs landing when lying in her bed, so she was aware if someone went into Luke's room or came into hers if she was awake. She always requested that her door be kept partially open after she was tucked in for the night, so we obliged and did so.

The following morning, I was busting at the seams, wanting to tell Brooke about my experience from the night before. I eagerly waited for her to wake up, so as soon as she started to stir, I sat on her bed so that I could visit with her for a few minutes. After catching up on a few things, I just let go.

I explained to Brooke exactly what I had witnessed and said that I thought that Luke must have seen his guardian angel, and without missing a beat, my nine and a half year old says to me, "Mom, I've seen him go into his room at night." Then she threw back the covers, got out of bed, and said, "He goes in like this," and in her childlike way of describing what she had seen, she starts to tiptoe.

Okay, right now, I am beside myself with such excitement, and I said, "Brooke! Tell me. What does he look like?" With not one hint of hesitation and with a little hint of it being a stupid question, she says, "Mom, he's made of light!" and then she says, "But I don't think that I am supposed to tell you this," and, just like that, drops the subject.

Children are so innocent and the way that Brooke just delivered her story with such detachment, as if it was no big deal, was simply amazing. I don't think that Brooke had ever really thought about what she had seen, yet it was triggered when I brought Luke's and my experience to her attention. But when I think back and remember seeing an angel beside my bed at a young age, it was no big deal to me either. This experience only intensified my belief in guardian angels.

I believe that children are much more receptive and in tune to anything that an adult might perceive as out of the ordinary because, for one thing, how do they know that something is out of the ordinary? They haven't experienced enough of life yet to understand that an experience like this not the norm. Plus, they are not weighed down by the responsibilities and the distractions of the world that come with being an adult.

Children are fascinating to watch and to listen to. You never know what might come through the mouth or the eyes of a babe.

PUBLISHING THE RHYME

I had never forgotten about the rhyme and, in fact, had never even recited it to my kids. I had one printed version of it, and it was tucked away somewhere amidst assorted notes, spiral notebooks, and writing pads, where I had jotted down thoughts over the last several years. These recorded thoughts were always in the back of my mind as something that I might be able to piece together one day for a possible self-help book because many of these thoughts had been so helpful to me along my path in life.

I have found that ideas come to me sometimes at the most inopportune moments for jotting something down. Many times, ideas come to me while I am taking a shower or driving my car or vacuuming our house, or they come to me in the middle of the night when I am half asleep. There must be a zone that I get into when outsides noises are muted. I have words written down on napkins, lists of things to do, sticky notes, envelopes, note cards, etc. Any piece of paper that happened to be available at the time a thought came to me became the choice item for a handy writing utensil.

I have never considered myself to be a writer because I was never good at composing book reports or let's say that I just did not like writing them. I would spend so much time trying to figure out how to even begin the paper, so English classes were never my favorite subject in school. I am also not a creative storyteller. I am really more of a note taker and a composer of thoughts and interesting experiences.

My note taking began in college when Wade and I first started dating. I jotted down short notes on annual calendars about things that took place, just about each day. I still record tidbits of information on calendars and have over thirty years worth of memories. These have come in handy when needing to remember the order of certain events when putting a photo album together or recalling fun experiences that took place during the year to talk about on our anniversary or at a holiday meal or when I found the books on the floor or the angel resting on the kitchen counter: August 12, 1997, and August 28, 1997, respectively.

Twelve years had passed and the seed was now firmly rooted in the soil and was starting to show signs of life. It was 2009 and I had just stepped out of my bedroom when Brooke, who was now a senior in high school, intercepted me in the hallway. She grabbed me firmly by the shoulders, looked me square in the eyes, and said to me, "You are going to write a book after I go off to college." I replied, "Really? What makes you say that?" Brooke shrugged her shoulders and responded, "I don't know…I just know."

I found her notably absolute comment—what I now realize was a message—very interesting because I don't know if I had ever really voiced to her my dream of writing a book one day because that was exactly what it was. It was a dream, a desire, an almost inner knowing, and it was something that I had kept to myself. Most of my note taking took place while Brooke was at school during the day, so what she experienced from me was my life as a wife and mother, a volunteer at school, a scout leader, a soccer team mom, a substitute teacher, and all that goes with managing our family life. My documentation of ideas that popped into my mind was sporadic, and Brooke knew that at times I wrote in a journal, but why would she voice that I would be an author one day?

2010 was the year that I found myself thinking about the rhyme a lot. Brooke was now in college and Luke was in middle school, so I had a little more time available to me. I was starting to feel restless. I had been a stay-at-home mom for nineteen years, and I was so ready to do something that was fulfilling to me and helpful to others and yet still provide me with the ability to be there for Luke. I had experienced this restless feeling several times over the years, but something made me want to pursue it further. So I sorted through my notes and papers and found the long lost, yet never forgotten about rhyme.

I sat down at my computer one September morning to search the Internet to see how to publish a children's book. My decision was that I would stir the pot, so to speak, and at the least, get the process going. I thought,

If this is supposed to take, then it will take. I just knew with no doubt whatsoever, that I was supposed to try.

I started with a publishing company that I was familiar with and read that they only accepted manuscripts through a book agent, which I did not have. My attention was then drawn to Tate Publishing's Web site where I read author testimonials and played videos. I liked what I saw and heard, so I asked them to e-mail me information, which I printed and put to the side. I was going to take time that fall to look at other publishing companies and compare notes and also see if I needed to get a book agent.

The very next morning, just as I was stepping into the house after dropping Luke off at school, the phone rang. I saw that Tate Publishing was calling me. I thought, *Seriously?* I picked up the phone, and it was a sweet girl who said, "We see that you asked us for information, so we are just curious if you have any questions." I was truly so surprised to get a phone call when I had not even requested one!

I wasn't really prepped for questions, but I explained how I had been sitting on a little rhyme for a long time and she said, "Just e-mail it to us. Let us see it and we'll let you know something in three to four weeks." So I happily cast whatever routine plans that I had made for that day to the side, and I found that perfect moment to type up the rhyme and send it to the publishing company. The only thing that I changed was the title.

I now called it *Angels Are God's Helpers.*

I was excited, yet I did not get my hopes up high because I knew that there was a slim chance that my little rhyme would be part of the three percent that are selected by the publisher on an annual basis. So I got on with my daily and weekly responsibilities and never really made the time to research other publishing companies during the next few weeks. There I was, letting the normal noises of my daily life take over to where I forgot about that amazing September day, even to the point to where I forgot to tell Wade about that whole experience.

It was early in October when I received that very important and completely surprising phone call. The publisher thought that my rhyme would make a sweet children's book, and I was flabbergasted, to say the least. The devil on one shoulder was poking me, saying, "Seriously, Shelly, it can't be that easy! There is something up with that." But the angel on the other shoulder was saying, "Oh, yes, it can…and now is the time."

"To every thing there is a season, and a time to every purpose under the heaven" (Ecclesiastes 3, KJV), and the season was now opportune for a divine gift from God to actually bloom into something very special.

LETTING GO AND TRUSTING THE PROCESS

It was time for me to step aside and truly let go and let God take control so that this incredible gift could flourish and thrive and be what it was supposed to be. Something beautiful was happening, and I certainly did not want to stand in the way and block the light that was needed for the development of this particular blessing.

This blessing was going to turn into a children's book, which made my heart so happy! I honestly didn't know what kind of book the rhyme would become or if it was to become a book at all. I just knew that I was supposed to try to make it a book, and it took with very little effort on my part. But as I am finding out, when God is behind a plan, the process will flow effortlessly when I don't try to control it. My job was to continue to keep my attention on God as much as possible and follow my inner guidance while maintaining peace and harmony within myself.

I did all that I could to take a backseat and let God direct this remarkable journey that was ahead of me. I wouldn't even go back to the publisher's Web site because I did not want anything to interfere with the flow. It felt right from the start. I knew that if I dug for more information and started to compare this publisher to another or read people's comments or opinions, that it was very possible that I could start to question my decision. And then doubt and fear could filter in and impede the process. So I chose not to dig because I did not want to chance it.

I was committed to seeing this divine gift through to its completion, and part of that commitment was for us to make a financial investment towards the book publishing process, so I had to trust that the money would not be an issue at all. As it would turn out, Brooke was awarded a financial scholarship, which meant that we had the money that was needed for the book, so it was unnecessary for us to have to stretch our wallet to make it work. That was another sure sign that the divine plan was in motion and that I was comfortably placed in the backseat.

I was assigned an editor in January 2011, and in mid-February, I received the e-mail of my manuscript after it had gone through the editing process. Opening that e-mail was one of the most nerve-wracking things I have had to do. I took a deep breath, and I said a silent prayer for peace and wisdom before I let myself see what was hidden behind the message bar. Once I was brave enough to open the edited document, I tensed up a little when I saw words highlighted in neon green.

Here I had a rhyme come through me word for word, I submitted it word for word, and it was accepted word for word. Now the editor had recommended that I change a few things about it. It was suggested that I direct it towards a child, such as change "our and us" to "your and you," as well as add five to seven more stanzas so that the illustrator would have something to draw from because I was getting ten illustrations with the book. Now it was starting to make sense on how it would turn into a children's book, though I was concerned about adding more stanzas. Was I supposed to change a divine gift?

That evening, something came up to where Wade and Luke had plans away from home, and interestingly so, I had the house to myself. That is not something that happens very often for me. It was obvious to me that I was being given an opportunity to talk and be mindful of the thoughts that came to me.

I turned off the television, and I sat on the couch with pen and paper in hand, and I said a prayer. I then said to God, "Give me the words. If you want me to add to this book, please give me the words that you would like me to say." Within an hour and a half, I had written down a few pages of ideas. The next morning, I started to piece it together because it had to be submitted within a couple of days, and I was really very pleased with the results.

Once the editing process was completed, the manuscript went to the illustration department. The illustrator was going to be selected by the publisher, so once again, I said to God, "You gave me the words for this book, so I trust that you will give the book to the perfect illustrator." I let it go and cast all worries or concerns to the side, and I took my focus off what might be going on with the book and stayed busy with my normal routine at home for the next several weeks.

Katie Brooks called me at the beginning of May and introduced herself as the illustrator for *Angels Are God's Helpers*. She made me get right down to business because we were now at the point where the book would pick up speed.

Katie and I discussed characters and ideas for scenes and she said that she would send an e-mail to me of what she was picturing in her mind, based on what we had discussed. I would see the characters in a couple of days, and I had one chance to make minor changes to hair color and clothing and such. After that, it was out of my hands.

As far as I was concerned it was already out of my hands because I had absolutely no idea what to expect. I had to have such great faith that God had this under control. After all, I had asked for the perfect illustrator so I had to trust that Katie was the answer.

This didn't mean that I might not be a little anxious about opening the document the day that Katie sent to me a copy of the characters, because I was. But I mustered up the courage and did it, and I was fine with what was originally created. After making a few adjustments, I was satisfied.

By the end of June, I was able to see what the completed book looked like. Katie did a wonderful job exhibiting the message that the rhyme conveyed and really was the perfect illustrator for the book. My heart was full of joy with the outcome. The publishing process just flowed and by August, I had my hands on the first hard copy of *Angels Are God's Helpers*.

Ten months had passed since I received the phone call of my dreams, and I now had a book in my possession that made a precious first reader for children, fourteen years to the month, after a little rhyme came to a busy mom, who was just making sure that the floors were clean in her home.

There has to be something beautiful on the horizon because this little children's book is just the beginning of a glorious plan that is being orchestrated by God.

EXTRAORDINARY QUESTION

The blooming process had certainly begun, and it was time for me tend to the nurturing and growth of this new gift that had been bestowed upon me. I was now its caretaker, and it was an honorable job to be given. It was absolutely like being responsible for the raising of a child, and I knew that my job would be to love this book, to care for this book, to give this book a stable foundation, and to support this book to help it to be the best that it could be. But like all babies, it didn't come with a handbook that had instructions on what to do.

Being a parent is an incredible job to have, and it is a most challenging job since there is no instruction manual included with the gift of a child. With the many trials and errors that come with this job, the main thing that I had learned by this time in my life was that I was much better at asking God for direction and paying attention to what my gut told me to do. I was more conditioned on how to be mindful of the roadblocks that could occur, so that I knew which pathway to take.

Thankfully, this baby was not going to keep me up at night and it was not going to huff and puff when it didn't get its way. I was not going to have interruptions that might exhaust me or demand my attention, so I was going to be able to pay closer attention to what my inner guidance told me to do. But I still had bit more to learn about the curious ways that God and guardian angels work.

So here I am with a children's book about believing in the assistance of guardian angels. The first copies came to me in August 2011, but it wasn't officially being released until November, so I could go ahead and start marketing it on my own to help spread the news of its impending arrival and availability in the market. I passed out many books, mailed books to friends and family, and set up a few book signing dates. I visited Tate Publishing so that I could record *Angels Are God's Helpers* and meet Katie Brooks, the marketing team, and the wonderful staff who had graciously helped me along the way with the publishing process.

September flew by, and by early October, I began to notice something interesting. By this time, I had passed out approximately fifty books, usually getting some sort of response such as "I believe in angels too!" or "This is so sweet!" or "Thank you!" I received all kinds of pleasant responses, but then, I noticed that a question was being posed right after I handed someone a book.

In every case, the person would glance at the book, smile, look at me, and say, "So, are you going to write another book?" I would always be a little taken aback and respond, "No, I have bits and pieces of other books written, but since this one is complete, I feel like I need to focus on marketing this book."

The exact question was posed time and time again, always at the same moment, with me giving people the same response. I said to Wade how I thought that it was strange that so many people were asking me if I was going to write another book. I compared this to visiting a new mom and her baby and asking, "So, are you going to have another baby?" It just would not happen!

As the month of October came to an end, I had an appointment set up with my chiropractor, so I took a book with me. After telling him a little of my story, I handed the book to the doctor, and he looks at it, smiles, looks at me and says, "So, are you going to write another book?"

I don't know how many people had asked this same question of me, but this enlightening moment was the exact moment when I first realized that divine messages could come through others. This was the moment when I realized that I needed to pay close attention to words that are presented to me, especially if the words or suggestions are repetitive and are constructive and helpful. I did not know this until this particular aha moment.

Never in my wildest dream would I have thought that an exact scenario could be staged, time after time, to get a point across. It was as if an angel was reaching through the veil, touching the person on the shoulder, whispering, "Ask Shelly this question right after you glance at the book because we are trying to get her attention on writing another book."

So I got down to business and I made time to focus on writing a book, yet I was still unsure what I should compose. I said to God, "What am I supposed to write about? Do you want me to write about my experiences? What am I supposed to do?" I was so apprehensive about telling my story, so I decided to try to create a story.

I thought that I would put together a sequel to *Angels Are God's Helpers* so that I would have two books to read to children when I went to the preschools. I started trying to make it happen and came up with another rhyme about angels, but I could only get so far before I would hit a wall and could not go any further. I then wrote about another uplifting experience that happened when my dad had passed away a few years prior and submitted it to the publishing company, but it didn't feel right to me just yet. During this time, the questions stopped being posed because I was trying to put something together, and I was back to receiving nice responses when marketing the children's book.

December came in all its busyness and glory, Brooke came home from college for the holidays, and I took a break in writing and marketing *Angels Are God's Helpers*. There were plenty of things to keep me busy during this time.

In mid-January 2012, Brooke had a doctor's appointment before she went back to school, so I joined her and took a book with me. I handed the book to the doctor and she looks at it, smiles, looks at me, and says, "So, are you going to write another book?" I could not believe it was happening again! Even Brooke commented on the curious question, which was now eleven weeks after the last seemingly staged inquiry.

It is needless to say that this time I knew what I had to do, yet I was still not quite sure what to focus on for the next book—that is, until I received an early morning phone call in late January from a daughter who woke up with an idea.

The idea was to talk about the unique experiences that I have had as well as the interesting stories that I had been collecting along the way. This same idea had been suggested by family and friends who knew of my experiences and also knew that I had been meeting people who had amazing stories of their own that they felt prompted to tell me about when they saw the children's book.

Each time, I had conveniently pushed their suggestions to the side because I was not comfortable about talking about my experiences to just anyone. But it was obvious to me now that this was the very thing that I was supposed to put into a book. I was being told in a way that only I could decipher, to be courageous and to step out and reveal information that hopefully will be helpful to others. Perhaps, this was going to be the book of my dreams.

I cannot imagine how many signs I have failed to notice throughout the years. I would have never realized that an exact question or recommendation could be phrased time after time in the same type of scenario, yet with different players, to get a point across. I now realize that I am given many opportunities to understand that the answers to my questions are right there on display. My own fears and limitations, control issues, and distractions of the outside world are what can keep me from noticing the answers, which may delay me from getting on the train that will put me on the right track. Hopefully, I haven't missed too many trains.

The remarkable ways that have guided me to this place where the words are starting to come together in the form of a book, helps me to know that this is precisely what I am to do. And when the train is chugging smoothly along the tracks, God is the great and divine conductor that is the One overseeing the direction of the train.

REMARKABLE GOD

*A personal journey to having an
unwavering relationship with God.*

Don't worry about anything; instead pray about everything. Tell God what you need, and thank Him for all He has done.

Philippians 4:6

TAKING OWNERSHIP

Perfect sense. It made perfect sense to me. I had to tell my story. Every time I handed *Angels Are God's Helpers* to someone, there was an intense feeling that welled up inside of me that made me want to explain more about how that little book transpired, which I found myself doing at times. There was a lot more that needed to be said, and by this time in my life, I knew that this was a feeling that I had to be mindful of. And because the feeling to do this might be helpful to others, then that serves a purpose that I know is helpful to God, and that feels right to me.

But how does one go about talking about something that is so mysterious, without drawing judgment, criticism, or condemnation toward oneself, when one lives in a world that is so very ready to strike and crucify another and pick one apart before they hang one out to dry? How does one dance this delicate dance without stepping on toes or challenging religious doctrine or putting the attention on me instead of on God?

This hesitation is what has kept me behind the scenes for a long time only sharing these extraordinary stories with a few close friends and family over the years. But now, it is as if I am being gently pushed forward from behind the curtain and out on to the great stage of life by supportive parents, who are assuring me that it is okay. "Go ahead, we've got you. Tell your story." And as I write *Remarkable Guidance*, it feels right to tell my story. I know in my heart that this is what I am supposed to do.

This confidence that I feel that I now have to be able to step forward has come after years of strengthening my own power cord connection to God. The connection that I used to have to God equated to more of a standard household extension cord connectivity level, and I have to talk about the process of how I did this because I want to convey that God is first in my life and that my believing in guardian angels is not about worshiping false idols. I am very aware that God is the One who is ultimately in control and I don't think that I would have been given a book about guardian angels if humanity did not have their assistance; nor would I have been given a publisher, which happened to be a Christian book publisher, to put the rhyme into print. The whole process has been divine.

This place where I am today, spiritually, is not even close to where I was in 1997. I have grown and evolved so much since then. Some may wonder why I didn't pursue a publisher when I finally put two and two together and realized that I was being encouraged to turn the rhyme into a book.

My answer would be that raising our daughter was my first priority and, also, that I would not have known how to give it all to God and let it go at that time. I wasn't there yet. I still had so many fears and insecurities, limitations and control issues in my world that would have prevented everything from flowing. The time was not right. The signs were just a precursor to what was ahead because God knew that I had some fine-tuning to do and obstacles to overcome before things could flow. I had to first walk through the forest, which has had its periods of dense brush as well as wonderful moments where light filtered beautifully through the trees, before I could get to the meadow where I would have a much clearer understanding of God.

Though I have been aware of God for much of my life, it took me years to truly have a relationship. Attending church was not a part of my life until recent years. The relationship that I now have with God is one that has been developed through an amazing process, and it has been through my own self-exploration, combined with my own assessments of the results of the life experiences that I have had so far that has lead me to where I am today.

Today, I am more at ease with my own self. Today, I am less fearful than I was in the beginning years of my life. Today, I am stronger and more confident and more secure with who I am. Today, I am more at peace, more harmonious, more joyful, more forgiving, more accepting, and more loving. I like who I am today, and I realize that I still have work to do on me, but I am better than I was before. I am still evolving.

My personal evolution began with reading self-help books or books about someone's personal account of how they rose above challenges in their own life or just

inspirational books in general. It was all so very helpful to me, and along the path, I have gathered tidbits
of information that have helped me along my path,
which helped me to strengthen my insecure human
self. I learned how to look more behind the scenes of
my own mental, feeling, and emotional worlds because
for whatever reason, I always felt as if I needed to be
better than who I was on the inside as well as be comfortable with who I was on the outside. There was a
driving force within me to do this very thing.

One super valuable tool that I used quite often
along my trek through the forest was journaling my
thoughts and my feelings. This survival skill came in
especially handy when I was going through an experience that was challenging to me. I am a quiet-natured
person and one who doesn't anger easily, and I have a
tendency to clam up when put on the spot. I needed
time to process and analyze words and circumstances
so that I could issue an effective response, if I felt it
necessary, so that I was not going back and saying, "Oh,
and here is another thing that I would like to point out"
or "Here's another reason why I feel this way."

I needed to get words and thoughts written down
and put into an orderly fashion so that I could weigh
out the pros and cons and the positives and negatives,
so that I could find the balance and a possible solution.
Then my response would make sense and this would
sometimes wind up in a most enlightening handwrit-
ten letter. Subsequently, I would feel better because I
knew that whatever I felt was needed to be said was
said in a way that might be understood by those who

were the lucky recipients of my thought-provoking composition of words and feelings.

The personal letters didn't take place all that often, but what did happen more regularly was taking the time to jot down my thoughts and feelings in a spiral notebook. I would do this mainly when I was feeling aggravated or bored or felt the walls closing in on me or when challenges arose that were uncomfortable in any sort of way.

I am someone who likes to be happy as often as possible, so any conflict that gnawed at my gut or went round and round in my brain is what I would eventually make time to sort out on paper when I had some quiet time to myself. When the moment arose, which sometimes I had to make happen, I would grab my trusty pen and paper and just write. I would usually start out with something like "It really bothered me when…" or "I am really tired of…" or "I am upset because…" and I would write and write not worrying about punctuation or spelling, and I would pour my heart out on paper.

The more that I wrote, the better I felt, and sometimes, what started off as a complaint about a current situation caused me to venture into experiences from the past that I didn't necessarily care for. Sometimes, the more that I dug, the further away I got from what I was upset about in the first place. This made me aware that just because someone else's actions might trigger a reaction out of me, that it meant that there were possibly unresolved issues that needed to be addressed. I realized that the challenges that I faced in my world wound up being more about me.

Through much trial and error, I learned that whatever bothered me didn't necessarily bother someone else. I found that when something caused me to feel angry or jealous or rejected or a host of many other unsettling feelings, that it was a reflection of something that was unresolved and still lingering in my world. Anything that bothered me was what I started referring to as "my stuff," and I learned how to own it because it was a part of me and my world. If something bothered me, it was mine to contend with.

Tending to my own personal "suitcase of issues" that carried my stuff was a process. At times, it was bulging at the sides due to an accumulation of negative feelings based on the results of issues that I had not properly handled, with many being because I was too young or immature to know how to handle at the time. It was scuffed up and marred a bit on the outside as well, but all of that helped to build character and strengthen me. It was all of the stuff that it was still holding on the inside that needed to be purged.

My suitcase carried all kinds of stuff such as issues of responsibility, limitation, rejection, lack, etc., which led to negative feelings of resentment, guilt, anger, jealousy, insecurity, unworthiness, etc. It carried results of negative experiences, which led to fear-based or judgmental issues, so I started to sort through and discard the negativity that was becoming such a burden for me to carry. I started to weed out the garments that were becoming a little too frayed or uncomfortable to wear anymore.

The thing that became very clear to me was that when I took the time to face any negative feeling or emotion that welled up inside of me, circumstances in my life got better. I noticed that whatever scenario was playing out, whether I was an active participant or not, started to subside or stopped completely.

This empowered me even more to take ownership of my stuff because I liked what I was seeing happening around me. I realized that my issues were being healed anytime I took the time to face the problem, whether I got to the root of the problem or not. I discovered how very important it was for me to not allow myself to become engaged in negative energy and to put myself in time out when I felt it necessary to do so. *Excuse me while I go rummage through my stuff*, I would think to myself, while I made an excuse to go the bathroom or something along those lines. Most of the time, it was just best to not say anything and to walk away when the time was right and hand whatever the problem was to God.

The greatest remedy to a conflict seemed to always occur when I dug deep enough to have the realization of what the source of the problem actually was. There was usually a core issue that may not have had anything to do with the scenario that played out. I found that sometimes one conflict was actually tied to other conflicts, and when I had that moment of realization of what the core issue was, it helped to resolve not just the challenge that I was going through, but others as well. Many times, just getting in touch with the core issue is what helped me to let go and let God.

During the summer of 1995, my dad was coming to town and was going to stay with us for a few days, and I was concerned. I loved my dad, but he was an alcoholic, so his actions were unpredictable, though thankfully, he was a sloppy drunk and not a violent drunk. Plus, he was barely making it by in life and might need money, so I just didn't know what to expect because it had been a while since I had seen him. I was concerned that something might happen that could be embarrassing or challenge us to dig into our limited bank account or create more uncomfortable memories.

I remember feeling stressed that night before Dad's four-day visit, and I sat on the curb in front of our house, after everyone was asleep, and just cried and talked to God. I had a lot of stress factors going on at that time: money issues, responsibility issues, exhaustion issues, as well as the impending arrival of my dad. I talked about some negative experiences that had happened in my youth, and I came to the awareness that a lot of the anger I was carrying was directed at my dad for not being more involved in my life. I thought that maybe some of the things I went through might not have occurred had he been around more. I realized that I did want to get to know him better and spend time with him, and I honestly did not care if he was drunk the whole weekend or if we covered all of the expenses of whatever we might do while he was in town. I just needed this time with him. I wanted this time with my dad no matter what.

Well, Dad stayed with us for those few days, and it was one of the best times that I had ever spent with him. Fun memories were created for me and my family, and I was reminded of the dad that I had loved as a child instead of focusing on the challenging experiences that came later. Dad never felt as though he needed to drink excessively and he didn't feel the need to ask us for help in financing anything for him. Money was even pitched in by family members to help with parking fees, gas, and food without me even asking for it. It was an incredible time and it just strengthened my relationship not only with my dad, but with God as well.

This was when I started to verbalize my thoughts and feelings more to God, though I did still pull out my spiral notebook at times as well. When faced with a challenge that was bothersome to any degree, I would separate myself and go for a walk or find a quite spot so that I could talk and ask for help. I would talk as if I was talking to an old friend, and I would unload what was on my mind, and I would usually get to a place where I was voicing what I wanted, which was something that was in my heart. It became more of "I don't like the way this feels!" "I am tired of feeling (rejected or insecure or frustrated or lonely or bored or a host of other negative feelings)," and I would turn it around and ask for the complete opposite of what I didn't want to feel anymore. "I want to feel (accepted or secure with who I am or peaceful or fulfilled or inspired, or a host of other positive feelings)." "I want to be happy!"

As I continued to own my stuff and work on me, my life improved in all areas: relationships, finances, health, opportunities, etc. Life essentially became more balanced, which helped me to become more balanced inside. This all helped me to look at the trials in my life as an opportunity to free myself from the burdens that were holding me back and keeping me stifled. I was happy to do so, even though it might be inconvenient, because I knew that by me taking charge of my issues that I was being released from the ties that were binding me.

As a result, my suitcase full of issues was becoming lighter, and I was becoming happier and more at peace inside. I was now very aware that my happiness was completely up to me. Whatever I perceived to be my challenge was up to me to seize. It was up to me to get rid of it.

It was up to me to give it to God.

DISCERNING FEELINGS

There is one constant in my life and that is one very reliable God. Everything else is fleeting. It's a temporary existence. I think about how, as people, we become dependent on others for our happiness, and if not others, we become dependent on things that make us feel good, which make us happy. But all of that is temporary, and then there's that void that needs to be filled again and then again. It's a never-ending process.

So how does one get out of that whirlpool of cyclical seemingly endless voids to fill and trials that life can bring? The survival instinct would tell one to look up and reach to grab on to something secure so that you can pull yourself to a place where you can catch your breath and rest for a while. But see, there is one of the key components to knowing God. A person has to decide to want to be rescued. The decision to want to rise above the whirlpool of challenges in life and create positive change is a personal decision. We are all ultimately on our own to make that choice.

Reaching up and looking for help is already instinctual and God is not a tangible source to grab on to. Our human brain tells us that the source would need to be tangible and that it would need to be beheld by the naked eye. You really can't fault one for not knowing how to rely on something that is not perceived by the majority of the five senses. We start out life being dependent on others who satisfy those innate senses that are needed for human survival for the beginning years of life. Then we leave the nest in search of our hopes and dreams, only perhaps to wake up one day feeling as though we have to be dependent on people and things to satisfy the physical senses, instead of testing the waters and issuing a request for assistance from God. We become dependent on others to make us happy.

I have tested the waters on countless occasions by asking God to please throw some sort of floating device my way, and it has been done so every time that I have asked for it to be tossed in my general direction. This is why I know that there has to be a God and knowing God takes practice. Knowing God is an experience. I have and continue to practice because the results make me happy and I like to be happy. It feels good to be happy, and it feels good to have my head above water.

But here's the fascinating revelation that I have become aware of through the years. I notice positive changes in the people in my life when I take the time to work on me.

This awareness leads me to believe that people subconsciously play roles for each other and that we are very connected on an innermost level—or perhaps it is on an uppermost level. I have found that the people who are in my inner circle best reflect many of my own strengths and weaknesses, so by me working on my weaknesses, the weaknesses are not reflected back to me through the people around me. And if they are, I know that I still have work to do on me. If I wanted to see positive changes in those in my inner circle, I needed to work on making positive changes within myself.

Plus, I feel as though we are all responding to the positive and negative vibes in each others worlds, so by me working on my own world, it was helpful to others around me. If anything, it was freeing them up from dealing with my baggage, which lessons some of my burdens that they might feel that they have to carry for me. I have taken it upon myself to play that role many times throughout the years when no one told me to play that part. I told me to play that part. It was up to me to change my role in the play if the part didn't work for me.

But changing my role is not necessarily about making an abrupt change. It is about changing what is inside of me, so that I can access what is still in my suitcase of issues. As I sort through my stuff I stay true to my personal mantra: *It's my stuff so let me deal with it. No one is responsible for my happiness. I am.* This helps to keep me focused on me. It is no one else's responsibility except mine to determine why I may not be at peace with something going on in my world. It is about me figuring out why certain negative scenarios play out, and it is about me facing the negative feeling that wells up inside.

I started to categorize my feelings and realized what I was working with here. The feeling has everything to do with whether the feeling is of the "light" or if the feeling is of the "darkness."

I have always been very sensitive to what feels right to me and what makes me feel uneasy. This is probably what catapulted me into my own soul-searching at an early age because I knew, at the very core of my being, that I just wanted to be completely happy—and I wanted everybody else to be happy too! The old saying, "If mama ain't happy, then nobody's happy," is so very true, but you can replace "mama" with every other important member in one's life. The world is a wonderful place when everyone in one's immediate world is happy.

Luke mirrors this need for everyone to be happy for me because he, too, is super sensitive. He has always been happy-go-lucky and just wants to have fun as much of the time as possible, and when Luke was three, he would eagerly meet Brooke as she arrived home after a long day at school. If she came home carrying the weight of the world on her shoulders, as she sometimes did, he would shove her while trying to push her back outside and loudly say, "Go away!" He could not handle her heavy mood. So like Luke, I just needed everybody to be happy, though I wasn't shoving anyone, because then, I was completely happy. And that is where I wanted to be as much of the time as possible.

That feeling of wanting to be completely happy and wanting everyone else to be happy as well, that was deep in the core of my being, was what I came to realize is part of the light. I believe that the light is of God, which is naturally joyous, harmonious, peaceful, giving, selfless, and kind. It is everything glorious, wonderful, and beautiful and is an abundance of all good things. It is true, omnipresent love.

The darkness is everything that opposes the light, and it usually does not feel good, though it can be deceptive. Negative emotions and feelings such as anger, jealousy, resentment, guilt, hatred, envy, loneliness, insecurity, unworthiness, selfishness, shame, rejection, etc., are not of God. I have found that these negative feelings, as long as they are paid attention to, will intensify in strength, which will cause the road to be pretty bumpy along the way. It works the same way when paying attention to feelings of the light, which leads to much smoother, unencumbered roads to travel.

My thought is this—that we are each a part of the light of God and that God's light is a part of each of us. I believe that we can see the light through a person's eyes and we can feel the light through a person's heart, but what can cloud the light within a person is all of their stuff—their own personal suitcase of issues, which is so very powerful and burdensome. It hides our true self, our true identity. It makes it hard for us to know who we are and hard for others to see who we actually are. I think that many people are crying out in their own way, "I want you to see me, not the mistakes that I have made or who I appear to be. Can't you see who I am?"

And God is the great "I AM."

All of that stuff is part of the darkness, and it is absolutely, positively, not part of the light. I believe that darkness is an accumulation of negative energy, and it feeds on those negative emotions and feelings, which accentuates the problems in one's world. It is extremely distracting because it attracts more challenges and roadblocks, and all of that keeps one from noticing what is good and wonderful in the world. It is that devil on the shoulder that can be very convincing and pokey with his pitchfork, encouraging one to remain focused on what is not right in one's own personal bubble. Darkness is sneaky and deceptive and ultimately downright uncomfortable once it has made its place in one's world. But all of that can come to a halt once one becomes aware that the power is within to take control of the bubble before the pitchfork causes it to explode.

Darkness is very real, and I have felt it's heaviness during extremely low times in my life, and I know people who have literally seen its menacing shadow. It is the very thing that can push a person over the edge and cause someone to do something that is so out of character for them. It is the very thing that can lead to such destruction of relationships, finances, health, jobs, etc. Darkness is the very thing that keeps people from being truly happy and at peace and free to be who they are here to be, and I believe that we are all here on a quest for true inner peace, harmony, and happiness— which is very freeing. And all of that is of God.

I have learned that if I avoid an uncomfortable feeling by letting too much time go by to where I forgot about what I was feeling in the first place, or I had a glass of wine or two, which led to the same result, then the negative feeling would resurface in a future setting. Many times, it would be a different scenario, with different players, but the outcome was still the same unsettling feeling. The more that I did not face the issue that was disturbing to me, the more that negative issue would become stronger, uglier, and nastier and much more uncomfortable to be around.

My big wake-up call happened during a time in my life where there was so much on my plate that I was not taking time to face my stuff. Basically, I wasn't handing enough over to God because I was trying to do everything myself. I was trying to make everybody happy, and the whirlpool of life was getting close to pulling me under because I was paying more attention to what seemed out of balance in my world and also, to that which made me feel stressed and unhappy. I was fueling a fire that did not need to be fueled and was essentially giving power to darkness instead of to light.

In addition to my life as a wife, mom, and manager of domestic affairs, I had taken on more responsibilities when my dad moved to town a few years prior. He needed more assistance with his life as his body was suffering the results of years of alcoholism.

I seized control of helping to manage Dad's life, and I made sure that his bills were made current and paid in a timely manner. I took him grocery shopping, to doctors appointments, and out for an occasional lunch. This was becoming a timely, laborious task because Dad was a large man, who was requiring more assistance with moving from point A to point B.

I had been visiting Dad on a weekly basis, and I was handling a lot, yet was carrying the weight of guilt, resentment, anger, and major responsibility issues, which all boiled down to the core feeling of never being able to have any fun. I was caught in a "poor me" low, depressed state of mind.

In addition to all of this, Wade and I had an argument before he left town for the week, and he had not called or answered my phone calls for three days. He was avoiding me like the plague, which for me, though I didn't realize it at the time, was one of the best things he could have done. He needed his space and I needed time to face the stuff that was getting too much for me to handle in my personal suitcase of issues. It was time for me to wake up and visually cast all negative feelings and fears into a raging bonfire and ask God for help.

I was standing in our kitchen late one evening after the kids were in bed, and I felt so very, very sad. In all of our years together, Wade had never failed to call and check in, and we rarely argued. That insecure part of me was afraid that our marriage was falling apart. I was scared. I was feeling so worthless, so burdened by the trials of life, so afraid of becoming a single parent and all that I knew could come with that role. I was almost as low as I could go.

I felt a heaviness that literally seemed to be pushing my shoulders down—a little bit of pressure, then a couple of seconds of rest, and then a little more pressure—all the while being saddled with heavy thoughts and feelings. I was so immersed in sadness for a few minutes that I was not paying much attention to the weight being applied until a thought came to me that shook me to the core. The thought was, *Things would be a lot easier if you took your life.*

Thankfully, I was awake enough to realize that I would never consciously think something so terrible, and I stood up with such a force, as if I was trying to get rid of this horrible darkness that was literally on my back, and I commanded it to "Stop!" I said, "You have no power over me!" I was determined to reclaim my personal bubble that the darkness had deviously infiltrated while I was too busy paying attention to the pokey pitchfork and words such as "Look how much freedom Wade has" compared to the responsibilities that kept me tied to the home; "Look at how he can cart away so easily," "Look at this," and "Look at that."

Well, it did stop, and for the next two days, I didn't care if Wade called me because I was determined to purge that accumulation of fear and negativity that I had been allowing myself to stay focused on. Every time that serpent tried to slither back into my world, I would meet it head on, with the same power of a lioness protecting her cubs from a dangerous predator, and I would command—in the name of God—that that darkness be annihilated!

I was adamant in my refusal to be afraid of it anymore or to believe the negative thoughts that were trying to cloud my mind. I knew in my heart that my marriage was strong enough to withstand rocky roads, and I felt confident that everything would be fine, however things wound up. Sure enough, the roads became smoother and my marriage didn't crumble. That soiled laundry was not bulging out of the sides of my suitcase of issues anymore.

That experience woke me up enough to realize how very important it is to stay on top of negative thoughts and feelings so that they do not accumulate, and to appropriately discern what is of God's light and what is of the opposing force. I refuse to allow myself to be "asleep at the wheel" because I have done that one too many times, so no matter what things appear like, I find something good to focus on. I make sure to look at things that I do like instead of that which I don't.

The shadow on the shoulder can be quite convincing and commanding of a lot of attention, and it took me years to wake up enough to understand how it works. It took me years to stop paying it any mind whatsoever, especially to words and feelings that pull my attention away from that which makes me feel at peace. Distraction is the name of the game, so instead of me allowing me to focus too long on anything that may ultimately cause me to feel disappointed that I don't have something that another might have—more of this or more of that; a better this or a better that— I distract myself with anything that nurtures the soul because it lifts the spirit and doesn't add to the weight of a suitcase.

When my kids were little, there were times where they seemed fussy for no apparent reason, so I would distract them with something that I knew made them happy. I would take them outside and point to a bird or a fluffy cloud or I would have them touch the bark of a tree and teach them the differences between the trees that we had in our yard or I would find a toy that they loved, and their fussiness would go by the wayside.

Well, as a wife of a hardworking, traveling man, and as a busy mom to two great kids, and as a dedicated daughter to an ailing father and to a wonderful mom and mother-in-law, I had to learn to stop looking to my husband or anything else to distract me from the responsibility load that was a part of my life. I had to learn how to go outside more often and look for the fluffy clouds. I learned how to put my attention more on God and my responsibility load felt much lighter and more doable. I became less fussy on the inside and Wade's travel schedule miraculously lightened up to where he was around a little more often during the week.

Life became more manageable when I started to be mindful of thoughts that could sway me off the path that was leading where I needed to be. I stopped comparing my suitcase to another's and became more aware of what was on the inside of mine, and I definitely stopped paying attention to the shadow on the shoulder. I started tuning it out because I was now well aware of what can happen if I tune in to the wrong channel for too long. It eventually becomes noisy and bossy and whiny, which can be aggravating and distracting and potentially cause me to give in. So I stand firm in my choice to be happy. I say yes to happiness and no to unhappiness.

It's like refusing to give in to a whiny child when you have already said no because you are confident that your decision is the right decision. Once the child realizes that you mean what you say, they stop trying to overpower you. And darkness does the same thing when you have made your decision to focus on something that causes you to smile and feel at peace.

Through the years that I have spent facing darkness that surfaces at times in my world, I have become freer and more empowered as I conquer it bit by bit. Every time my internal radar goes off, I meet it before it has a chance to settle and make itself at home because I am determined to not let it ever get to a point where it could fester and possibly overcome me and my world and all that is a part of it. I choose to stand guard and protect the light inside of me that the darkness would prefer that I not even realize is there. I am in control of my own world through God, and I know that the light always prevails and will lead me to a place where I am ultimately happy and at peace inside.

This unwavering determination to be free from all insecurities, all limitations, all selfishness, all fears, and everything that is disruptive to my inner peace is what has helped me to discover that the golden key to remaining free from anything that could cloud the light inside of me, is to ask God for forgiveness for all that has gone before.

And I mean everything.

PERPETUAL FORGIVENESS

Freedom is another thing that I think we are all searching for. Freedom, which comes with inner peace, happiness, and harmony. No one likes being told what to do and I think that we start rebelling as soon as our soul is confined to the limitations of a human body. I know that I tense up when I feel as though I am being put under a little duress by someone else's standards of what they think I should do or be. I think that I have always known inside that I want to operate from my heart and not from my head. It just took me a long time to learn how to do that. Freedom, to be who I truly am and to live the life that I have come here to live, which ultimately leads to happiness. "Life, liberty, and the pursuit of happiness." Hmmm, very interesting indeed the way that came out of my head to put on paper.

One crucial part of owning my stuff was accepting that whatever I perceived to be my issues and whatever negative challenges were playing out in my world were there for a reason. I can analyze the heck out of it and I have, but I have resigned myself to knowing that only God knows for certain what the basis to my own struggles are truly about. I accept that many of the reasons are possibly the results of faltering along the way.

"But wait! How can that be when I am a nice person and a rule follower and I have always tried to do my best with what life has handed me?" which was my way of thinking for years! Well, it all comes down to owning everything and that means completely accepting that whatever is or has been in my world, from the start to the present, has all been there for a reason. If it is in my suitcase, then it is mine to seize, so therefore, it is mine to give to God because only God knows what is truly behind the source of any situation, any circumstance, any behavior, any seemingly random falling of the dice.

God is the pathway to freedom.

I see God as a loving, forgiving, extremely patient, and supportive, authoritative figure, and I think about how I should react when I know that I have faltered, which is the same expectation that I have of my kids when they knowingly have broken the rules— 'fess up, say you are sorry with meaning behind it, and ask for forgiveness. So I started to do that very thing, not that very long ago, even though whatever I was experiencing might not have seemed as though I was at fault.

It is easy to point fingers, so I started to point more in my direction and not so much away from me because I am very aware that I have made mistakes, and I am very aware that I have made mistakes that I wasn't even aware of at the time that I made them. I have handled situations inappropriately. I have swept things under the rug out of fear of confrontation or not having enough faith in myself. I have pacified others to keep them at peace while avoiding the issue that needed to be addressed. I have selfishly looked the other way, thinking that people would wake up after enough knocks on the head like I did.

God knows that I haven't been the perfect wife, mother, daughter, sibling, or friend, but the thing is God also knows that I now recognize that my ways of handling people and life has, at times, been inadequate. But I am making efforts to be an all-around better person, and I honestly think that that matters to God. Whatever it is, I accept that any unrest that may be in my world is perhaps there because of mistakes that I have made, knowingly and unknowingly. I take complete responsibility for what could be the results of the errors of my ways. I own it.

This awareness really came to me when *Angels Are God's Helpers* started to become a reality. It was then that I took a closer look at the words that came through me in 1997. For thirteen years, those words remained hidden in the back of a closet between piles of paper that I was saving for what could possibly become a book one day, and I was drawn particularly to the part of the rhyme that says, "They do not judge, criticize, nor condemn/They want us to see the good in all men." So I pulled out my trusty dictionary and looked up the meaning of those three words: judgment, criticism, and condemnation, and I became aware that this was a terrible cycle that had kept me mired in certain conflicts for a long time. Those three words are usually in cahoots with one another.

I interpret that part of the stanza as God saying that in order to see the good in all men, people should not form an authoritative opinion or find fault or blame others. This enlightening part of the rhyme helped me to become my own jury and access that I was guilty on all accounts and realize that it was time for me to make changes within myself and to be very conscious of my actions. It was extremely necessary for me to rein in that part of me that might want to point fingers.

The experiences in my life have afforded me many opportunities to wake up, and this was one of the most illumining revelations that I have had. This was a major aha moment for me, which caused me to look deeper into my particular ways of being.

Though I have never been an outwardly judgmental person, I have had thoughts that were judgmental, and I now know that my thoughts are being paid attention to. I know that I have expressed my opinion many times when I didn't need to do so, and I now know that my words are being listened to. I know that I have held other people responsible for my problems, even if I didn't verbally express it, and I now know that my feelings are being monitored as well. And when I think about the many times where my insecure self felt jealous or envious or allowed myself to get involved in negative gossip or acted selfishly or thought that I knew better or was better or whatever, I realize that I have failed in innumerable and perhaps shameful ways.

There is no telling how my judgments or words or reactions or even inactions have affected my world or other people and their worlds. I have no idea what may have been set into motion by things that I have thought or said or done. I just know that I want to be forgiven for everything because I was not awake enough at that time in my life when I made beds that weren't tucked in nice and pretty.

But thankfully, I am now more conscious. Conscious enough to realize, that anything that seems to be out of sorts in my own world might be because of my own doing, and I want to undo what I may have created for me or for others. I want to smooth out the wrinkles in those beds because I am honestly tired of reaping what I may have sown. I have enough on my list of things to do, so I stopped pointing fingers and got on with my list and started to iron my own sheets.

I have asked God for forgiveness off and on throughout the years, but now, I am just more thorough with my ironing. I press harder into those stubborn wrinkles, so anytime a negative feeling wells up inside of me, I ask God to forgive me for whatever creation is behind that negative feeling. Anytime that I have a negative or judgmental thought that flits through my mind, I ask God to forgive me for having that thought. Anytime that I knowingly respond poorly to anyone or any situation, I ask for God's forgiveness for that particular scenario.

The more that I do this, the more harmonious my world becomes, and the more aware I am that asking God for forgiveness is extremely healing for me and for others as well. Asking God for forgiveness is the key to freeing to the soul. "Forgive me for whatever is behind this challenge—this feeling—this dark cloud that is looming in my world." "Forgive me because I do not want this anymore!"

As I became more mindful of the power of forgiveness, I noticed that I would occasionally have a remembrance of something that occurred years ago, and many times, there wasn't anything that would have even triggered the memory. I would think how strange it was that I was even thinking about that particular past experience, but in every case, it was a memory of something that I did not handle well at the time.

I feel as though the past experiences were being brought to my attention so that I would ask for forgiveness for them. This really is encouraging to me because I believe that I am being freed up from past misdeeds and I know in my heart that I am doing the right thing. So I keep at it, and I know that I am forgiven because God knows that I truly want to be forgiven. He knows that it is in my heart for me to be forgiven. The proof is in the peace and harmony and happiness that I am feeling and noticing in my world.

I now own everything, including the mistakes of anybody who played or currently plays a part in my life because I am tied to them on some level. Whether it is an emotional or physical or spiritual tie, their world may have an impact on me and my world, just as mine may have on their world, so I ask for forgiveness for all that has gone before for that person as well no matter what. This especially goes for my immediate family because there is no telling how my own fears, judgments, limitations, control issues, and such have negatively affected my kids or my husband, so I own their stuff too.

I remember a time several years back, when a mom said to me that she wished that she hadn't judged other mothers for letting their children use pacifiers because now she had a child who she wished would take a pacifier. She'd give anything for that child to take a pacifier.

This is a minor example of "What you put out, you get back," which I have seen play out many times in my life. I think that life has a way of helping us see why people do what they do, so I stopped questioning other's motives and circumstances and just tried to pay more attention to mine. Life's constant boomerang effect has very possibly affected the people I care about the most, hopefully more positively than negatively, but still, I take responsibility for the negative stuff.

This reactionary world with its cause and effect implications is what I am trying to rise above, and forgiving myself and forgiving others is the true golden key. Forgiveness is what releases and cuts one free and helps to lighten one's personal baggage. When one's baggage is lighter, it helps one to be more forgiving of others, which helps to start the purging process of household closets.

When it comes to cleaning out an actual household closet, not all of the stuff in there is necessarily mine, but I still take it upon myself to clean it out because it feels good to me to have that closet in better order. I no longer care about waiting for others to get their stuff out of the closet before I get to work on it because it feels good to have it off my list, which makes me happy and therefore the feeling of happiness filters to those around me, which hopefully helps them to feel happy.

Figurative household closets have been cluttered and out of order since way before recorded time, and many are born into households that haven't been kept tidy. That is why it is so important to forgive others because honestly, I think that in most cases people are doing their best with the knowledge that they have at the time they are going through the experiences of their life. It doesn't make it right necessarily, but it is the world that we live in. And it is an imperfect world full of imperfect people carrying suitcases that are sometimes overwhelmingly stuffed with negative issues and fallout, which can cause such damage—not just to one's self, but to others as well. The closets in people's lives get very cluttered with stuff.

It's easy to go there and say, "I'm not cleaning out this closet because most of this mess is not mine," and in the meantime, the mess keeps piling up because of time constraints and such and the stress levels rise because now the list of things to do is going to take longer to accomplish. Well, someone has to clean out the closet. Otherwise, it stays on the back burner and never gets done, which leads to other closets filling up until it all just gets to a point to where it is unmanageable.

Forgiveness makes it more manageable. Asking God to forgive another for whatever is behind the negative challenge going on in their world helps to lighten another's baggage so that they are freer and things become clearer. Then maybe they can start staying on top of their own stuff and eventually keep their own household closet organized as well. It begins a positive domino effect in someone's life, which is so much better than the negative domino effects that create stuff.

I think about how for years I allowed someone else's opinion of how I looked or walked or talked to affect me negatively. I also think about how my junior high years were a very short time in my life and how a little segment of time can create a negative domino effect in a person's life. Who knows what the girl who liked to bully me was going through in her own life? Well, let's see—God knows. So I ask for forgiveness for her so that she is cut free from any guilt that she might carry now for how she reacted to me then. She might not even realize how I allowed her actions to affect me, but I still ask for forgiveness for that just-in-case scenario.

My mom would say at times, "If you remember it, then you haven't forgiven it," which took me a while to truly understand. Then one day, I started to turn the tables with anyone who I had issues with in my life, and instead of looking at the negative scenario that played out and the negative results that remained in my world from that negative scenario, I looked at what I gained from those experiences. So with my junior high friend, I looked at how I eventually learned how to speak up for myself and how I have compassion for others, no matter what they look like or how they walk or talk. And I can thank her for picking on me because it strengthened me in more ways than one.

I had a stepfather for a short time in my life who overstepped his boundaries one day and harshly punished me, when I really didn't do anything to warrant such behavior. The results of how that impacted me played out off and on in my life until I said to God, "Cut me free from whatever this is because I do not want to feel this feeling like I am being punished when I have always followed the rules. Forgive me for whatever is behind this creation."

As time went on, I slowly learned to completely forgive my stepfather. I learned to turn things around and found things that I could thank him for such as teaching me how to play tennis, which gave me an outlet in high school because I was good enough to be on the tennis team. All of that helped me to come out of my shell and have a group of friends that helped to build confidence in a very shy girl at that time. So I learned to say, "Thank you for teaching me this or introducing me to that," and it changed my heart, which changed my world.

I have pictured in my mind at times, how I might react if I noticed any players in my life walking up the sidewalk to my front door. What feeling would well up inside of me when I saw who it was? Would I open the door and welcome them inside and perhaps offer them a glass of sweet tea or would I pretend that I wasn't home? How I might feel gives me a gauge on if there is anything left in my suitcase of issues. If so, then I still have work to do on me. Things take time, and God knows that there can be a lot to sort through. I am now at a place where I would welcome my stepfather into my home and it took me a long time to get to this place. It took me a long time.

I find myself in a perpetual state of asking for forgiveness for anything that seems amiss in my world because I have a lifetime of mishandlings and who knows how long that might take to undo. But I am happy to utilize a whole lifetime of asking for forgiveness because God knows that I do not want to carry that stuff with me when I meet Him beyond the pearly gates of heaven. I want my suitcase as empty of dirty laundry and worn-out garments as possible, so that I am able to hold my head up high as I stand before Him in His glorious presence.

Things that use to bother me don't play out in my world anymore. I don't even remember what used to aggravate me. It has been difficult for me to come up with examples of past challenges as I write this book because so much has been healed in my world. The bandages covering those old wounds are too adhered for me to pry off to see what was underneath. I know that it is not necessary for me to go back and dig up any of the negativity that used to be there because it is not healthy for me or for anyone connected to whatever the scenario may have been.

Humbled by the power of God's grace, I am being released through forgiveness, and I am becoming freer to move forward less hampered by past transgressions—whatever they may have been.

CONSCIOUS

I think back to the late 1970s and early 1980s and how my girlfriends and I would intentionally get sunburned so that we could tan faster. We would put iodine in our baby oil and slather our skin with that concoction, and then lie on reflective mats or float in the middle of a swimming pool for that souped up, attractive sun ray effect—oblivious to the damage that we were causing our skin. What was I thinking? I wasn't thinking! I didn't know better then, but now I do.

Well, such is life, full of its trials and errors, its ups and its downs, its giant learning curves, and its opportunities to become more conscious of God. Living life on Earth is like being in a classroom environment with God being the divine instructor, and I am now that eager student who has learned a lot in the assorted required studies, but now is driven more to do my very best with life instead of just coasting through. I have had enough strength and conditioning classes and sunburned moments that make me determined to strive to move forward and to learn from my mistakes. I don't want to go backwards or even stagnate for too long. I am now more driven by consciousness—a consciousness that comes from being conditioned to be dependent on God alone.

The one thing that I have control over in this world is my mind. I am responsible for me and who I am. I am in charge of my happiness, and by doing that, people in my life are happier, which makes me happy. Life is ultimately an individual trek so I have to be conscious of my thoughts, the words that I speak, my actions, and where I allow my attention to go.

My many years of experience in this grand classroom environment have taught me important tactics that are now so helpful to me, and many have to do with where I put my attention. My mom would say to me at times, "Be careful where you put your attention because where your attention is, you are." Her words help me to stay focused on what is right and not what is wrong.

I have learned that if I focus on being concerned about not having enough money, then things tend to break down to where I have to spend more money, which will only intensify my concern of not having enough money. Or if I am focused on not having enough time to accomplish things on my to do list, then more busyness tends to be created, which gives me less time to accomplish the things that are on my list. I have found that life really does work this way, so I am now more conscious as to where I put my attention and things seem to work out fine and fall into balance.

I now know that it is important for me to take my attention off of anything negative and put it on to something positive—"Like attracts like." If I focus on things that instill positive feelings, I tend to attract experiences that make me happy, and if I focus too long on things that instill negative feelings, I tend to attract more setbacks.

The challenging part to this very simple reality is mastering that part of me that might be distracted by negativity, so I control what I can control, such as turning off the news if I feel like it and turning on music that lifts me and makes me feel joyous. It is not that I am tuning out and putting blinders on, but I am tuning in. By tuning in, I am more aware and more on guard and I am able to be more conscious of what feels right and what feels wrong.

I am more present with God.

Getting to this place in my life where I am paying more attention to trying to be a better student of life meant that I needed to stop trying to do other people's homework for them. That was an easy role for me to fall into because I care about people and want them to be happy, so it was easy for me to want to help others see what I have learned in certain subjects. I have provided many words of wisdom so many times in the past, which I feel was helpful at times, but much of the time, the words were wasted. And sometimes, the role that I put myself in became burdensome.

There was a time years back when a friend told me that I was carrying another friend's burden for them. I had been doing what I thought a friend should do when another needs to vent, so I would listen to this friend and the troubles that she was going through, and I would let her unload her stuff on me. I would provide her with ideas that could perhaps solve the challenges that she was going through and she would feel much better and then call me within another day or so to unload her stuff again.

I had been doing this for months, and I did not realize how I had been enabling this friend who felt as though she needed a shoulder to lean on until I heard those enlightening words from my other friend. When I truly got that I needed to stop being so available, I felt physically exhausted for three days! It was just as if I had been bearing the extra weight of an actual physical burden.

That was a big eye-opener for me because it taught me how to be helpful without taking on another's burden. I learned to ask God to help with the burden of another, instead of trying to carry theirs along with mine. I realize now that by allowing myself to be a crutch for someone that it could delay another's ability to face challenges and ultimately stand on their own feet, so that they could move forward in life. So I ask for forgiveness for anything that I may have done to hamper another's progress because only God knows what course of study will be best for their development.

The courses of study come in increments and are so perfect for the molding and transforming of a person to give them a form of knowledge that another might not have. Those forms of knowledge are what lead us to eventually provide a service that is helpful to life which is helpful to God, which is life.

Our paths are unique and specific to our purpose and depending on how one manages the moments where one stumbles and falls, as well as the obstacle course that might need to be conquered before one reaches the fork along the path, will determine which direction one chooses to take. The directions are not necessarily good or bad, but I think that there is always a path that is a bit smoother and will lead in a way that is fulfilling to the soul. All paths nevertheless lead to having a better understanding of God, if one chooses to look at the brighter side of things.

These moments where decisions need to be made are moments where it is helpful to be conscious of God. And to be conscious, it helps to not have too many distractions that can inhibit what one needs to be able to recognize, so that they can go in the direction that feels right to take.

Life is full of numerous distractions and so many ways to get out of balance, which can lead to many moments of setbacks and stumbling along the way. When there are too many distractions, it is hard to be conscious of what path to venture on; or decisions are made for the wrong reasons that put one on a path that is not leading the way that might be necessary for whatever the soul is here to do. Sometimes, life's gentle nudges become more of a push, and sometimes, life will actually shove one onto a path that leads in a better direction. That shove actually took place for Wade and me in September 2008, and it was downright uncomfortable for a while afterwards.

By this time in our life, we had invested in beach properties after spending years venturing to the beach to visit family. Our first investment was a little one-room cabin that we had purchased when Brooke was five years old. It sat two doors down from my mother-in-law's retirement retreat and it had a wonderful front-row view of the Gulf of Mexico. Wade and I poured a lot of love and labor and money into bringing that cabin up-to-date over the years, replacing the roof and pilings, adding siding to the outside and walls to the inside, extending the deck, and so many other smaller updates. It was initially fun, but life was starting to get labor intensive.

The problem was that we decided to add two additional properties to our already long list of responsibilities. The thought was that we would refurbish these houses and put them up for rent at some point, and the money that we could make would help put our kids through college. One property was added in 2004, and we called it "Brooke's Tuition," and it sat on the third row in the same neighborhood. The other was added in 2006, and we called it "Luke's Tuition," and it sat on the second row. For four years, those properties held our attention, adding such stress to our lives, weekend after laborious weekend.

The house that we called "Luke's Tuition" was the one that took so much of our attention. We purchased it in an as-is condition and its internal condition was dire, at best. The appeal to this house was that it sat on an oversized lot with a fantastic view of the ocean from its second row vantage point. We rented a dumpster because we literally had to gut the house. Everything from its twenty-year-old carpets to its ceiling fans to its maggot-infested refrigerator was hoisted over the railing into the dumpster. The purging process was fulfilling, but the months of renovation started to take its toll.

Beach properties require a lot of care because of the salt-air environment, so what started out as a fun use of time became what my mom had warned me about, and the beach properties literally held our attention "hook, line, and sinker." We had to finish what we had started. We were in so deep with so many bills to pay, so many projects to focus on, and so much time being dedicated to packing up the truck and hauling things back and forth to the beach on an at the least, twice a month basis. All of this on top of Wade's travel schedule and my busy life of managing our lives as well.

One weekend in July 2008, we had finally finished updating all of the properties, and we had friends staying in each of the beach houses. We stayed at Wade's mom's house and invited our friends to join us on the beach one evening. We built a bonfire and it was a glorious night. The sky was clear, the moon was reflecting on the ocean, there was a gentle breeze, and laughter was in the air. I remember feeling so relieved to finally be able to relax enough to enjoy the fruits of our labor, but it was a feeling that would only last about seven more weeks.

In September, a giant storm brewed in the Gulf of Mexico, and it was one that I knew would pack a punch so hard that it would leave a mark, and it was headed our way. We had seen a lot of storms throughout the years, but this one was ominous and it seemed driven to wreak havoc along its path.

Hurricane Ike pummeled the Texas coast, and the Bolivar Peninsula took the brunt of the impact from that Category 4 storm, taking with it the three investment properties, Wade's mom's house, and about 3,300 other homes and businesses as well. Most of the houses literally floated away like bumper boats, being herded to what would become a massive, 13 ½ million cubic yard debris field, leaving not much more than broken pilings and concrete slabs behind.

Everything in life happens for a reason, and having a portion of a slate practically wiped clean was a blessing in disguise. Once we got through the trauma of the loss and all that went with it and the health challenges that showed up due to the stress levels, we could finally breathe and live a simpler life. It was nice to be back on track focusing on that which was essential instead of being so distracted by busyness.

The beach houses and all of the stuff inside them were meaningless in the grand scheme of things, though I do wish I had that jar of a few hundred shark's teeth that had been collected throughout the years by our family. Thankfully, we have our lives and pictures to remember the fun times that we did have there together as the memories and time that we share with others are priceless and much more important than a glass container full of tiny beach treasures.

Life is full of defining moments and impactful times like these cause you to hang on tight, attempt to keep your head above water, and exercise a tremendous amount of trust that you will land on your feet somewhere along the way. There is no telling what path the giant wave of life is going to place you on, and sometimes, you land on a path that will lead to a grander purpose.

When the impact of the giant wave that crashed into our life finally settled down and started to recede, I found that I had my feet planted on a path that I needed to explore.

COMPLETE SURRENDER

2010 was the year that many things in my life took a turn for the better. That was the year that I threw in the towel. Though I truly had balanced out so many areas of my life by this time, I still had some major stuff acting out in my world. I finally had reached a point to where I was done. I was starting to get a little crispy around the edges.

I said to God, "You take it. It is yours. I trust that you will take care of everything and I will accept whatever is ahead, because I know that you have me and all concerned in your best interests." And I let it go. I completely surrendered.

The main thing that the experience of losing so much in one fell swoop had taught me was that my faith and trust in God was undeniable and I knew that everything would be fine, no matter what the outcome was. I could not let fear hamper me anymore. I realized that I was still trying to control certain things to go the way that I thought things should go. I did see positive results in the past when I put myself in charge, but many times, the results were temporary. I was still trying to captain my own ship and captain other people's ships at times, so I surrendered. I just let go. I completely acknowledged that I was not the one in charge anymore.

The biggest ship that I had been trying to captain was my husband. Wade was a heavy drinker, and I lived with a fear based issue of him ultimately becoming an alcoholic like my dad, with me possibly becoming a single parent like my mom. I tried hard to convince Wade that he could control his tendency to overindulge because he had proven on many occasions that he could do that very thing.

The bottom line was that I did not want him to be an alcoholic because I thought, *I'll be dadgummed if he has an addiction that infringes on my fun.* That was my core issue. I wanted the freedom to be able to enjoy a glass of wine together or entertain friends, as we had done on countless occasions throughout the years. I wanted that date night at a romantic Italian restaurant to still occasionally happen. I wanted what I deemed as fun because it really had been fun for the both of us many, many times.

The problem was that I was playing God and was trying to make Wade be who I wanted him to be. I was fighting for him to not be defined as an alcoholic, and I finally realized that my efforts of steering his ship was not working out so well. It was time for me to relinquish the helm.

When we first met in college, Wade and I were involved in the Greek life on campus, which meant that there were a lot of parties that kept us entertained. My calendars from those days remind me how much drinking keg beer or trashcan punch was such a huge part of our young life at that time. It was a big part of my branching out days, though I learned how to not overdo it. On the other hand, Wade had a hard time controlling that part of him that sometimes knew that he needed to stop before things got out of hand. "Just one more," the devil on his shoulder would say, "just one more."

Wade's greatest challenge was that alcohol was very available to him through his line of work. Things were pretty good for most of our years together, but I noticed that there was a pattern developing where Wade would stop drinking for a while, then he would pick it back up, and a couple of weeks later, there would be one of those nights that was absolutely not fun—for me at least.

Those incidents were getting darker because Wade was getting angrier at himself for not being able to control his actions. Plus darkness feeds on people when their defenses are low and the attention is kept on thoughts and feelings that oppose the light. All of that darkness was getting pretty heavy and pretty scary, and I was seeing a man who I loved become someone that I knew he was not. I knew Wade's heart, and by this time in our life together, his heart was not happy, and it had been that way for quite some time.

Well, I finally had enough. I gave. I could not do this anymore. My strong, caring, determined, stubborn, and ultimately selfish personality could only carry so much. I came to the awareness that I had been trying to control things to keep from being hurt on so many levels, not just for me—but for Wade, for our kids, and for our families. I was trying to protect everybody and that was applying so much unneeded weight to this human body. It was time for me to scale back the amount of suitcases that I had been carrying to just mine, and those who were not capable of doing so just yet—my kids. It was also time for me to resist all temptation to revisit any negative scenario from the past because Wade had enough of his own stuff to sort through.

By completely surrendering, while at the same time asking for forgiveness for anything that I had done to keep Wade mired, because trust me—I know that I played a part in that one—it was as though whatever fear based idea that I was holding on to was dislodged. Now the floodgates were open wider, and the blessings that had been building up behind that barrier started to be released. Life began to flow in a seemingly effort-less manner.

One of the big life-altering events that happened in our life early in 2010 was that we started to go to church. In the twenty-four years of marriage as of that time, attending church had never been a part of our weekly ritual. The excuse that we had always used was that because of Wade's very busy travel schedule, we wanted to have the weekends to sleep in, give Wade a chance to accomplish household chores on his list, and spend time together as a family.

Life worked fine that way for us for a long time, but the excuses were starting to wear thin. It was time for something to strengthen the foundation of our life, which was developing stress fractures that could not be kept up with.

My renewed self was going to go whether Wade went with me or not because by this time, I had stopped waiting for others to climb aboard a boat that was leading in a direction that made me feel happy. I was starting to live life more for me while still being responsible for the commitments that I had made to love and care for my family. I needed to be around fluffy clouds because I was done with trying to make a dark heavy cloud become light and billowy. Time was of the essence, and I knew that I only had so much time to do what I felt like I needed to be doing.

The middle school years were fast approaching for Luke, and I found myself praying one morning for him to have a great experience in sixth grade. I had always prayed for our kids to have teachers and classes that they enjoyed before their next school year, which always led to good results. I was getting a head start on this request because usually by February, Luke was stressed by the repetitive testing that goes on and would verbally express his discontent with having to go to school, which was stressful for me.

That very afternoon, I called a friend to say hello, and she just happened to be picking her kids up from a private school at that very moment. She told me that her kids absolutely loved their new school and I thought how I would love to hear Luke say how much he liked going to school. Private school had never really been on my radar as a possibility because we were zoned to good public schools. I decided that Wade and I should explore that potential endeavor since the idea had been presented to me so quickly.

The exploration process was successful, and we knew immediately that private school was the route to take. It felt right to us, and we knew that Luke would benefit from its many advantages such as smaller classrooms and less standardized evaluations.

Being affiliated with a church was a necessary requirement for enrolling in private school, so that was the very thing that pushed us into a church environment. I will never forget the overwhelming sense of joy and peace that I felt when standing in the sanctuary during a service at a nearby church, and I could not stop the tears. Talk about life beginning to flow! I knew that I needed to be in a place that had an amazing positive energy because life had been pretty stressful with its giant shove onto another branch of the river of life. It was most definitely what Wade needed because once he made the decision to test the waters, his life began to flow as well and his days became brighter.

After attending a few services, Wade learned how to stop trying to lug his suitcase by himself. He finally learned how to forgive himself and how to allow himself to be forgiven. Wade's early church life had taught him that he was responsible for any misdoings and that he should feel guilty and carry that guilt in his suitcase. And being the rule follower that he is, that is what he did for a long, long time. By the end of 2010, water, sweet tea, and lemonade became his drinks of choice, and Wade was so much happier, which made me happy.

All of these positive changes were beginning to happen during the spring of that year, and that is when I felt an intense prompting to write. I found myself waking up and wanting to write my thoughts down, and I did this every day for two weeks straight. Thoughts that I had jotted down off and on for years just poured out until I had to go out of town one weekend. Then I returned to my normal routine of managing our lives. I thought that I would pick the writing back up when I had more time, but apparently, I needed a little nudging because it was time for another extraordinary sign.

I kept a pen and pad beside the bed to jot down ideas that came to me during the night and one morning, a month after I had put my writing aside, I got out of bed and was about to step into our bathroom, when I noticed the sign. The pen that had been sitting on top of the writing pad on my nightstand was now perfectly placed in the center of the carpet right before I would enter our bathroom. It was now about five feet from where it had been originally placed.

Once again, Wade was out of town on a business trip, so he was not the responsible party. It was an obvious sign for me to get back to writing. I was thrilled! So I did start writing again, and it was in the fall of 2010 when I was prompted to just try and see if I could publish the rhyme that came to me in 1997. Then I put my writing to the side to focus on the publishing process of *Angels Are God's Helpers* and then the marketing of the book before I started getting questions about writing another book.

For a reason known only to God and my guardian angels, I was being guided to escalate the process of putting a book together and to stop procrastinating and to resume writing. The most recent extraordinary sign and the words coming through others were filling me with a sense of necessity for me to get back to work and to stick with it. God knows that I need a little pressure behind me to put things at the top of my list, and writing this book became a major priority for me to keep in that very spot.

This book is a dream of mine, and I am in complete wonder and awe of God in how I even got to this place. Many of the thoughts that I have written down throughout the years have been gently woven into this book. I have been guided in a very remarkable way to be in this very place, writing this very book, at this very time.

This is what has been in my heart to do for years, and the time was now for this desire to begin to transpire.

HEART'S DESIRE

I was thinking of our cat, Coco, while I was vacuuming our house this morning. I was in that zone again, and I was thinking about issues in general and I thought about how our cat had major issues for the first thirteen years of her life.

Coco is a calico that we got for Brooke when she was six years old. Brooke really wanted a dog, but we already had two house cats that were our babies before Brooke was born. They were great cats who ventured outdoors at times, and I did not want to deal with the responsibility of caring for a dog because I was busy enough as it was. So we agreed to have another cat.

Brooke wanted a cat that was white and had a pink nose. We heard about a calico in the neighborhood that had kittens, and one of the kittens was a calico with a white face and a pink nose. She was the closest cat that we could find that would meet Brooke's specifications. What we didn't pay attention to was that this kitten chose to hide behind the dining room hutch when we went to retrieve her. There was not one social bone in her body. It turns out that Coco was terrified and pretty much stayed that way until we forced her outside after Brooke went to college.

We were replacing the existing carpet with new carpet in our home, and it was time to train Coco to be an outdoor resident. Coco had developed a terrible habit of marking the inside of the house as her territory because of a tom cat that would woo or taunt her, during the wee hours of the morning. Being jolted awake by her terrifying screams at times, were hard enough, but Coco's repetitive use of our home as a form of communication was a bit much.

For two weeks, we refused to give in to her pleas to let her back inside of the house. She finally gave and realized that deep inside of her heart, she had her own desires. Coco figured out what her true calling was in life and she was happy. She now hunts and catches birds, lizards, dragonflies, and grasshoppers while still bucking for a few treats and pets. She is fulfilling her heart's desire in her kitty sort of way.

I use Coco as an example because she had to break past the fear-based barriers that she had grown up believing was so. She believed that she had to be dependent on others for her comfort, for her survival, and for her happiness. The temptation to venture inside the house is gone and she will even sit outside during a heavy downpour, instead of hiding amongst the indoor jungle of furniture and closet corners, like she used to do when she heard a raindrop hit a window. Coco is freer to be the cat that she is and she is so happy!

Breaking past the responsibility and fear-based barriers was a huge release for me. Those were major hurdles for me to overcome successfully, which enabled me to be freer to move forward so that I could start fulfilling my heart's desire. My heart had told me for many years that I wanted to help inspire others to work on themselves, if they wished to see positive changes in their world. I wanted to inspire others to find happiness.

Managing beach properties was more of Wade's decision than mine. I went along initially with it because it seemed to make him happy, but I did it for the wrong reason. I had unknowingly put my dreams aside, and as time went on, it seemed as though I was getting further away from being able to do something that was empowering to me.

The loss of the beach houses had taken its toll on Wade, and his way of coping with the stress had gotten so far out of hand. I had to completely surrender and let go and trust that all would fall into its perfect place, whatever that perfect place was. I finally let go of that branch that I had been holding on to for so long and let the current of the river of life guide me to where I needed to be. I had to be completely at peace and flow. I could not resist anymore and getting to that place of having such faith was what opened the door for me to start to fulfill a desire that was in my heart. It was a purpose that I knew deep down, that I had to strive for. I wanted to strive for it.

This desire that I have had to write a self-help book came way before the rhyme. I was unsure how I would follow through with making this book a reality. I just knew that it was something that I intended to try to do after my kids became more independent. I knew that

I had to be busy doing something with my time once they had their own lives to live, so that they were not feeling responsible for me and my happiness. I had no idea at the time that I would focus so much on talking about God, but as I have discovered, talking to God is the pathway to complete happiness.

I now realize that all of the years that I have spent whittling away the layers of stuff on my quest to find complete happiness led me right to the core, which is my heart. Each time I faced the feeling or circumstance that was aggravating to some degree or another, the weaker it became until all that was left was a puff of smoke. Once the smoke cleared, I have become much more aware of what my heart tells me to do. I am more conscious of what feels right to me.

If something doesn't feel right to me, then it usually means that I need to go another direction. It is kind of like having a pebble in my shoe that needs my attention before it causes a blister. I know that I should stop and cast the pebble aside and ask for direction. I don't try to make things happen like I used to do, and I am more aware of the inner promptings that I feel. I let God direct me, such as when I make a phone call to someone, I will try a couple of times, and if I don't get right to them, I know that I am not supposed to talk to that person, at that time. If I run into too many walls, then I know that I need to put my focus elsewhere.

When *Angels Are God's Helpers* was first was released, I put my focus on approaching churches. I really thought that since the book was a divine gift that the route would be through church organizations, but that was not as easy as I thought it might be. Public schools were out of the question because "God" is displayed on the cover of the book, so because I felt like a wind-up toy trying to find the small space that would lead into the next room, I knew that I had to put my focus elsewhere. I said to God, "Help me to know what I am to do. Help me find the best way to market this book."

The month before the book's release date, I joined Wade on a business trip to New York City and the surrounding states. I took books with me so that I could donate them to a children's hospital while we were there. I wound up leaving them in Hartford, Connecticut, and it felt so right to me! I loved the feeling of being helpful and I absolutely loved knowing that many children would be receiving such a special book!

Once the book was released, I set up a few book signings, and while that was fun, it still didn't feel right to me to stand behind a table and sell a few books here and there. It was taking a lot of my time to do this, and that was when I realized that I should donate books to children's hospitals. I had to trust that the money would be there to purchase the books, so that I could keep getting them into the hospitals, and the hospitals would make sure that the books got into the hands that needed them the most. I wanted God to flow through me because my path was going to take much more time, and I was going to get more pebbles caught in my shoe.

Since then, I have donated hundreds of books, with the goal one day of having donated thousands of books to hospitals. This brings me such joy to have a way of being helpful. It is something that I truly do love.

Operating from the heart is what feels good. It feels so right.

The heart represents love, and I believe that the true feeling that is deep inside of the heart is of God. As I have stayed on top of darkness, my heart has become bigger and less guarded by my suitcase and more guarded by consciousness. And by opening the entrance into my own heart, things that instill feelings of joy and love manifest in my world more readily, and that has ultimately increased my love for God, for humanity, and for life itself.

Love is the answer. Love is God.

I unknowingly tapped into my heart a few years ago, when I made time to put in writing that which I wanted to have on a vision board one day. I planned to clip out words and pictures from magazines to adhere to a poster board things that I would like to see manifest in my world. I thought—What makes me feel good? What makes me feel happy? What do I enjoy doing? What am I passionate about? What do I love?

I wrote down things such as I love spending time with my family and friends, beautiful outdoor settings, the soothing sound of a flowing stream, live music, and I love to laugh. I wrote that I love books and I love the serenity of being surrounded by books in a bookstore or library. I wrote things such as I love a happy house with the joyful sounds of kids having fun and a husband who is less stressed about work and finds more time to play. I wrote down things such as I would love to have a job that puts me around people who are honest and inspirational, while still having time for my family. I wrote that I would love to make money to help lighten the financial load on my husband, make sure that my adventurous mom could travel freely, be able to take a spontaneous trip to visit family and friends, as well as be helpful to others in many wonderful ways.

I jotted down so many different things that I know bring me peace and joy and would help me to feel content. The thing was everything was subjective. Nothing was specific. Everything that I wrote was what I know makes me feel happy inside. Everything that I wrote was or would be fulfilling to me.

I never made time to clip out pictures from magazines to put on my vision board, and when I started pulling my assorted notes together for this book, I happened upon the list and realized that a lot of what I had written down had already manifested. It was so amazing to me, but really, not very surprising.

The secret was that I took the time. I turned off the noise and the distractions of the outside world and I listened to me. I listened to the desires of my heart and my heart said, "This is what truly makes me happy." I was communicating with God while being very unaware of the power of making a heartfelt list.

Living a life that is full of happiness is about taking the time to talk. It is about making the world around me come briefly to a halt so I can determine what truly brings me joy. It is about following what my heart says, and as long as it is of the light and is good and honorable and is not self-serving or spiteful, it should be just fine. It is about mustering up the courage to stand firm and refuse to believe in anything of the darkness and to stop paying attention to that shadow on the shoulder. It is about making amends and asking for forgiveness for everything that has gone before. It is about giving up and letting go and allowing God to be in the driver's seat because I was too tired to drive anymore.

I am determined to remain victorious over the darkness that can cloud the light that is in my heart. And by standing on guard and paying attention and not allowing myself to get too distracted or become complacent, I keep the light inside of me bright. By protecting the light inside of me, the light of God becomes more powerful in my world, and I walk much taller with a feeling of peace, happiness, and love, a sense of purpose and confidence knowing that all is well—because it is. I refuse to believe it otherwise.

Living life with joy in my heart helps to keep the darkness at bay because darkness does not like a happy heart.

GRATEFULLY PRESENT

My years of being a relentless searcher have lead me to this place where I have a greater understanding of life, though I know that there is still much to learn. It is as though I have finally made it to the meadow and I am now stepping out into the clearing, and it feels amazingly liberating! I feel so much lighter and more at peace and happier and less weighed down by the trials of life. And though it took a long time for me to get to this place where I am living life more from my heart than from my head, it has been worth every step of the way. It has been worth every sacrifice to be here holding my suitcase, which is not as scuffed up as some and is more scuffed up than others, but it is tough on the outside and it is comfortable on the inside—and that is what really matters.

My suitcase is balanced and is now decorated with angels, smiley faces, hearts, and pretty flowers—beautiful vibrant colors, and things that make me feel happy and at peace. This suitcase is mine and I am proud of it. It represents me. It is who I am now and it is who I am still becoming.

I look back at the forest with such gratefulness for all that has gone before. I appreciate every person, every experience, and each gentle push to giant shove that got me here to this place, to this meadow. It is all meaningful in such a deep and profound way to me now. I see more clearly how people and events have helped to mold and transform me in ways that have made me stronger, more resilient, happy, and at peace. This is where I want to be. I do not want to go backwards. I want to only live for what is now and I want to only move forward.

I am so thankful for the challenges that I have had in my life because I was catapulted into a state of determination to rid myself of issues that weighed me down and made it difficult for me to advance. I know that the challenges that I have faced have always strengthened me in one way or another making me a better mom, wife, daughter, and an overall better person. And because of the years that I have spent conducting my own soul searching while working on my own fears and insecurities and limitations, combined with the extraordinary experiences that I have had, I have a deep and profound connection with God and my guardian angels.

Every step has been a benefit to me, to raise my own awareness as to what works and what doesn't work for me in my world. Every step has helped me to understand my own strengths and weaknesses so that I could find the balance—that cushy spot in between where I was comfortable. I wouldn't change anything in my life because without the great highs and the great lows and all that was in between, I wouldn't be where I am today.

Today, I do my best to not worry about anything that comes my way. Trials will arise because that is the nature of life and life may even play hardball at times. But I have had enough conditioning to know that I will walk more confidently and courageously through the storm because I know what to do with anything that challenges my feelings. I know how to put on the suit of armor of the light of God, and I know how to rise up and ask for help. I know how to ask for forgiveness for myself, for others, and for whatever creation is behind any challenge. I know how to stand firm with a knowing that because I have asked for help, that the help is being provided whether I can see it or not.

This is where I am today.

Today, I live completely in the moment. I live for this day alone. I am no longer the insecure person who dwelled on mistakes of the past or got caught in what could have been or what should have been, and I am not that person who used to worry about what might be ahead. The past has served its purpose for where I am currently today, and for that I am thankful, and I really haven't the foggiest idea about what is ahead—though I do believe that there has to be something so extraordinary that is truly beyond comprehension, somewhere in the foreseeable future.

Everything depends on how I handle what is at hand now. My world is about this day, and it is a daily walk and it is a daily talk. This day is enough to take on.

The negative voice tries to haunt me more these days by pointing out the aging and gravitational effects going on with my body, which can be almost terrifying at times. I try to immediately redirect my focus to things that make me smile and things to be so grateful to God for such as "Thank you for this body that still functions and carries me forward" and "Thank you for the warm shower and for the money to be able to purchase products that help to ease the aging process." The thing is, I don't want to give anything that seems imperfect power anymore. I just want to give God power.

There is something to expressing gratefulness, and I think that it is because it is a recognition that it is not me that is the doer. It is an acknowledgment that there is a power that is so much greater than me that is truly in control. By formulating words of thankfulness, either verbally or through my thoughts, or just looking up towards the heavens and smiling, it is a way of tapping into the source of all life.

The feeling of being thankful comes through the heart and the heart is what expands God's light. When there is a natural flow of love through the heart to God and the heart is open to receiving back the glorious gifts of the light, then that is how God's blessings come into play in one's life. And that is what helps one naturally desire to be loving and helpful and giving and encouraging, etc., because that is God working through them.

I think of how I feel as a wife and a parent when thankfulness is expressed through my husband or my children. Though they may not see or realize the work that went into helping their lives to be as comfortable as I could help them to be, with my limited resources, energy, and time, my heart expands when gratitude comes forth. When it does occur, my heart just wants to do more to bring happiness to them. It makes me want to continue doing what I am doing and possibly do more as well because it is empowering to feel that the efforts that I put forth are meaningful and worthwhile. Though I don't look for these expressions, it always helps to build the light within me and that filters back out into those around me, and I think that God works in similar, more magnificent ways.

I can only imagine how God responds when gratefulness is expressed with a genuine feeling behind it because God's power is limitless and God is a power that is so positive, and everything that is sustainable, meaningful, and worthwhile is found there. I have and continue to see it work in my world.

Through God is protection. Through God is healing. Through God is supply. Through God is security. Through God is forgiveness. Through God is happiness. Through God is love. Through God is peace. Through God is harmony. Through God is who I really am, and I now know that I am worthy of any of these gifts of God and many more that are provided as well because my suitcase is balanced enough for me to see the glory of God.

Today, I live in a constant state of gratefulness and appreciation and love for God. No matter what seems to be going on around me, I choose to see something to be so very thankful for. I acknowledge that God is a part of everything good and constructive because without God, I wouldn't be alive for this particular day because God is a part of me. So I begin each day with a smile on my face and feelings of gratefulness, knowing that I have another opportunity to move forward and try to better myself and be helpful to others. Without God, I wouldn't have the sun to brighten my day or air to breathe or food to eat or water to drink. Without God, I wouldn't have clothes to wear or shoes to put on my feet, so I live each day with feelings of gratefulness for everything good and constructive, meaningful, and sustainable. Without God, I wouldn't have a roof over my head or a place to rest my body at the end of the day, so I close each day with gratefulness to God for the day that was just completed. Without God, I would not have the privilege of living this life and have this wonderful opportunity to try to become a light in what can be a dark world.

Living life with feelings of gratefulness for everything good and meaningful in my world is what really works. Living life with a relentless abandonment and love for God is the secret. This is what keeps life flowing in an unencumbered way. This is what attracts the perfect people, the perfect circumstances, the perfect timing, and the perfect scenario—which always leads to the perfect outcome.

Keeping my attention on God while consciously maintaining peace and harmony within myself, even in the face of that which is challenging and discordant in nature, is what ultimately works!

So as I live in this current moment and I am thankful for my computer and for the minds and hands behind this very helpful creation; and I am thankful for the table that supports the computer and for the bubble wrap that helps to keep my wrists from getting sore; and I am appreciative of the comfortable, peaceful surroundings while I think about what I am writing and for the sunshine coming through the window and for the sound of the baby mockingbird outside, crying for more food, I am living in the now. That way, I can stay present.

And by being gratefully present, I am much more in tune with God, and it is a place where I want to be as close to one hundred percent of the time as I can get.

REMARKABLE STORIES

A compilation of God and angel-driven experiences.

Angel of God
My guardian dear,
To whom God's love commits me here;
Ever this day
Be at my side,
To light and guard
To rule and guide

Old English Prayer

COMMUNICATION

I don't have all of the answers to the problems in life and I don't presume to know it all, but the thing that I know for certain is that it works to talk it out. It works to communicate all frustrations, all fears, all worries, and all concerns, and it works to communicate all that makes my heart happy. "This is what I want—more of this and less of that—and I thank you for helping me with this."

Communication is what helped me to realize that I had stuff that needed to be addressed. It helped me to eventually learn how to lighten my suitcase of issues, which helped me to follow my heart, which helped to open the door for a bigger purpose to be revealed.

Communication is what helped to open my eyes to see and to have an understanding that help is available because the more that I talked and asked for assistance with life, the more that I became aware of the assistance. The more that I became aware of the assistance, the more empowered I became to never cease communicating.

Communicating is the pathway to happiness. It is the pathway to freedom. It is the pathway to harmony and to peace and to love. But it takes time to truly understand that it helps to communicate as often as possible.

The old days found me asking God for the day to flow well for me and my family on about an every three-day basis. Things would go so well for those days, to the point, that I did not take the time to ask for the current day to go well because everything was flowing and people were happy, which always made me happy. Then something would happen that would create stress or frustration of some sort, which would cause me to wake up enough to make time to talk to God. I would ask for help with whatever challenge was going on in my world or those in my inner circle, and things would get better for about another three days.

Well, all that it takes is to have enough knocks on the head and enough wake-up calls to start making it a daily talk. And then the daily talk becomes a many times a day talk, and this is where it all is. It is a constant communication, a constant expression of gratitude, a constant awareness, and a constant connection and love for God.

I never wanted to add another ounce of weight to another's burden, so my tendency was to climb into my shell when I was frustrated or irritated or just tired of certain conflicts. Many of the challenges that I have faced had to do with other people being unhappy. This is perhaps why I now have a children's book about knowing that help is available and to just talk and ask for the help.

The more that I talked things out, the more the issues that I was contending with started to resolve so much that the issues were no longer a factor. The less that I had to contend with, the clearer everything became and the more aware I became of the assistance of guardian angels. The ones who are kind, patient, and full of light and love and are here to assist us from way up above.

The ones who brighten our every day.

REMARKABLE ASSISTANCE

"Ask, just ask!," is what I want to say when I hear someone voice a concern or something that they are worried about. Ask for the scenario that you would like to see instead of worrying about whatever negative scenario could play out. Worrying is, many times, the result of challenging past experiences, and this is one of the very things that can keep the same negative or challenging scenario playing out. This can keep the whirlpool of negative experiences circulating. This can keep people mired in the same, seemingly, ceaseless scenario. I say this because I know this. I have walked this route many a time.

Say that you have a relative who is coming for a weekend stay, and it always has been an uncomfortable experience for you. Naturally, you are worried that you will have another uncomfortable experience. Ask God to take out of your world and your relative's world whatever is behind the negative drama that can play out. Ask for forgiveness for whatever is behind the root cause of the agitation. Ask for peace and for great conversation and for joy for all concerned. Ask to be so very happy with the outcome of the visit. Just ask, let it go, and know that your request is being taken care of. When you notice that things are working out and possibly even going better than you may have thought, say, "Thank you."

My dream has been a desire to inspire others to understand that there is such assistance with life just by talking and asking for help. I would love for there to be an understanding that you do not have to get to a point where you are on your knees pleading for God's help. All of the help is through asking for the assistance when you feel that you need it, so that you don't ever get to a point of desperation. It is an everyday, worthwhile, immensely valuable form of communication.

For years I have talked everything out with God and then, almost as easily as "poof," I have been appointed to be the custodian of a book about guardian angels. If I were to decipher what this is all about, I would say that God wants people to know that assistance is available anytime you ask and even when you don't ask. It is about knowing that you are not alone on this earthly journey and the power is in recognizing this and to be comforted with that very knowledge.

I know people who don't want to bother God with the little things in life. They think that He has way too much on His plate already than to bug Him with their minor issues. So they don't talk at all unless things get pretty challenging in their life or they just save it for larger requests. The rhyme that came to me is all about guardian angels assisting us, so I like to think of them as loving family who patiently wait for me to give them an assignment and are happy to help me out when I do. The help is always there and many times it is right there to be seen, sometimes when I didn't even ask for the assistance.

Recently, I was focused on replacing the car that I had been driving for a few years. I was ready for a car that would more efficiently carry cargo while I was out marketing books. After conducting a little research, I narrowed down my choice to two vehicles that I really liked, yet I had not made time to see them at the dealerships.

Immediately, I started noticing these two vehicles everywhere I went, when I had not really noticed them before. It was as if I was being given many opportunities to compare the two while I was out and about. There was even a day after exiting the grocery store and right there before my eyes, with nothing obscuring my view, were the exact vehicles under consideration. They just happened to be the same color, with the same trim, and were parked nose to tail. I took a few minutes comparing the two at a closer range and I made my decision on which one I would focus my search.

I knew that I wanted a used vehicle with low mileage, so after further research, I wrote down the year, model, and color choice that I would keep an eye out for. Within the same week, Wade was searching online to see if he could find something close to what I was looking for, and his attention was drawn to the exact car that I had jotted down on a sticky note. The vehicle just happened to be in our city and it had less than 2,000 miles recorded on the odometer! The next day, I wound up with the car, and it even had a place for me to store books that I like to carry with me. It was just perfect and was priced considerably less than cars that had much more mileage. It was more than I could have even hoped for. It was divine.

Experiences like this only confirm to me that my human self is not the one in charge and has never been the one in charge. Divine experiences happen all of the time and I am now more aware of the assistance that is available. I know that the angels are there, even though they are not visible to me. I think that it is this way because life is already distracting enough with all that is visible and because it would be too easy to become completely dependent on them instead of on God.

Acknowledging the help that is there expands my heart and fills it with love and appreciation towards God and my guardian angels for helping to guide and protect me along the way, even when I wasn't aware of the help that was provided to me then as I am now. But now is what is most important.

Living in the now is where the power truly is.

I can imagine the angels saying, "Let us help you with this. Don't struggle. Just ask," and I can imagine how the angels happily get to work when given an assignment that is going to be helpful to the one who asked, especially if it has merit. I can also imagine how they would stop and patiently wait when the one who asked for help starts to worry and doubt what they have already prayed about. This, I believe, is what slows down and possibly halts the answer to a prayer.

I can imagine the love that the angels send back to someone who said a prayer for another to help lift that person above the challenges that are going on in their life, so that they know what to do. And I can imagine the love that the angels send to those who are helpful to another, especially when it comes from a place that lies within the heart. I realize that this is all imagery, but I believe that the angels of light are full of God's love, and God's love is boundless and immeasurable.

God's way is infinite and my brain, which is so finite in its thinking capability, cannot even conceptualize how perfectly things work out when I ask for guidance or for help or for the day to flow well. I just know that it works to talk and many of my conversations begin with "I thank you for helping me…think clearly/ be productive this day/know what I need to do in this situation" or "I thank you for seeing that…I don't hurt myself when working on this project/I don't catch that bug that I was just exposed to/I don't ruin my shirt," such as when frying bacon or adding bleach to a load of laundry.

So I ask for help with things such as trying to find something that I have misplaced or to remember something that I might forget because I am not where I can write the thought down on paper. I ask for help so that I don't make any mistakes when I am working on something, so that I get it right the first time, like hanging a picture or signing a book or cooking a meal. I ask for help in knowing if I need to say something to someone who is going through something trying and, if so, to give me the right words that would be helpful to that person. I ask for help to clear a space for me on a busy freeway, so that I can safely move over into the lane that I need to be in.

I ask for help with so many things, and I see the results of the assistance provided to me, and it is always good. It might not be what I would have envisioned, but when I try not to make things to be what I think they should be, there seems to be a peace, fluidity, and a balance, which is comforting. It is all so very heart warming.

I believe that my guardian angels are the ones who prompt me to suddenly look at the clock and realize that I have to leave right now to pick my son up from school or to remember that I have an appointment to keep. I believe that my guardian angels bring to my awareness that I have something cooking on the stove that I had forgotten about or my attention is brought to an electrical cord that is about to be a fire hazard. I believe that my guardian angels are the ones who alert me just in time to avoid a collision with another car or to realize that I should take the next exit because the traffic is piled up just ahead.

I believe that a lot of the prodding and prompting that I feel is from my guardian angels. I know this because it is not my conscious mind that has that sudden jolt to become aware of things. There is something much grander at play. Many of the promptings that I notice I believe are God-driven and angel-driven. It seems as though I am constantly saying "Thank you," either verbally or in my mind. "Thank you for getting me home safely/for getting me here on time/for that wonderful person who was so helpful/for that great idea/for that perfect parking space/for helping me find a bathroom before it is too late!"

I have learned that life truly is a daily walk and it is a daily talk, which leads to my "daily bread."

Every day, it is about acknowledging that God is the One in control and asking for guidance and protection for me, for my family, for our friends, for their families, and for anybody we meet along the way. It is about asking for the divine plan to be fulfilled in whatever is going on because then, it is what God knows will work best for everyone concerned.

Every day, it is about asking to be led the right way, to have everything fall into its perfect place, and for the day to flow well. It is about asking for help in making good decisions, to encounter people with good intentions, and to give me the right words to say, if I am to say anything at all.

Every day, it is about asking for meetings and appointments to go smoothly, to have time to accomplish that which needs to be taken care of, and that it works out for me to spend quality time with my family. It is about asking for balance, peace, and harmony, and to be happy at the end of the day with how the day transpired.

Every day, it is all about asking for the glorious hand of God to be present in all that takes place, up and down and around every bend in the road travelled that leads toward the meadow.

Each and every day—just ask!

REMARKABLE SIGN

It was July of 2006, and I received a phone call from the skilled nursing facility that my dad was living in, that he was being transported to a hospital for what seemed to be a precautionary visit. The staff didn't seem concerned, and by this time, Dad had been in and out of hospitals so many times that it had become almost a routine. So I decided that I would visit him the next morning instead of meeting him there that evening.

Sadly and extremely unexpectedly, Dad wound up passing away during the night. For days, I was riddled with guilt that I chose not to go to the hospital and that he died alone. At times, I would talk to him and say, "I know that you are at peace, but I just need a sign."

Two days before we had the memorial service for Dad, I was backing my car out of our driveway, and I noticed a small yellow balloon nestled next to our home. The first thought that came to me was "I wonder if that is a sign from Dad?" I then quickly brushed the thought away, thinking that it was a pretty silly thought, and later that day, I realized how special that balloon actually was and that maybe I was right after all.

The balloon was not much bigger than the palm of my hand, and attached to this yellow balloon was a rainbow-colored yarn with a neon orange-colored card stock in the shape of a sun. On the card stock was a child's handwriting that said, "For the wages of sin is death, but the gift of God is eternal life" (Romans 6:23, NIV). On the back of the card stock was a note that said to "Please send back to FBC /New Roads, Louisiana."

I was lifted! The sadness that had been weighing on me was gone. I was so excited about the idea of contacting the church and letting them know where the child's balloon had landed and how the balloon came at a time when I needed it the most. I knew the chance of someone actually receiving a balloon and taking time to write back was slim, so I could hardly wait to let them know where it had found its final resting spot.

In August, I wrote a letter and enclosed with it, the deflated balloon, along with notes that my family had written after the memorial service. Hoping to receive a response back from the church, I added a note at the end of the letter inquiring when and where the balloon was released because I was curious how long it took for it to travel to our home.

A month passed by before I was pleasantly surprised to receive a response to my question. The letter was from Mrs. Fulmer who went into great detail of how she had chaperoned a group of students to DeRidder, Louisiana, for a youth camp. She said that there were a handful of kids who really preferred to be with the older students who went to a camp in Tennessee, and one of these was a twelve-year-old named Henry. He had been having a difficult time transitioning into the youth group, so Mrs. Fulmer had been praying for something to inspire Henry.

On the last day of camp, the students got together to release balloons to help spread God's word. Mrs. Fulmer explained how she only had enough helium to barely inflate the fifty-seven balloons needed for the coordinated launch. Of the many balloons released that day in July, there was only one that the church received back, and that was Henry's balloon—the yellow balloon that lifted my family.

A deacon at the church shared my letter and Henry's experience with the Sunday morning services, the Bible study groups, the youth group, the church choir, Awana, and the children at First Baptist Church. He even submitted the story for an article in their small town newspaper. Our story combined with Henry's story was such an uplifting experience for so many people!

Mrs. Fulmer said it perfectly in her letter that September day: "God really wanted to speak to all of us. He touched your family in a special way with awesome timing. He taught the children that He can use even them. He taught me to let Him handle all things. He taught Henry that He really is paying attention and that Henry has value. Most of all, He showed us all that despite weather, helium, trees, distance, fear, regret, mourning, and time, He is *always* in control and that the truth written on that orange card is so important, He provided a way for multiple families, generations, and communities to be exposed to it."

Henry's balloon travelled approximately 220 miles in somewhere between 12 and 18 hours of time. I think that it would be scientifically impossible for it to travel as far as it did in such a short amount of time without coming to a halt somewhere along the way. And when I think about the size of the balloon and how it was perfectly nestled next to our home and not our next-door neighbor's home or the one across the street, the more I feel that an angel brought it to me—or maybe it was my dad after all. I really don't discount that theory at all, not with the extraordinary experiences that I have had.

My prayer combined with Mrs. Fulmer's prayer resulted in the lifting of a grieving daughter and her family and an almost teenage boy, as well as a little town in Louisiana, in a way that only God can orchestrate. On top of all of that, it turns out that Romans 6:23 was one of my dad's favorite verses from the Bible.

God has innumerable ways of answering our calls, and I was shown loud and clear how He was listening to me that summer day in 2006. That little yellow balloon was truly a remarkable sign from above.

The stories are everywhere and each of the following stories have come from people who I have met along my path in life, with most being brought to my attention while marketing *Angels Are God's Helpers*. Many felt encouraged to tell me their story when they realized that I had a story as well. Some of the names have been changed and some names I never knew.

I pray that I have done justice to the stories that people have shared with me as the experiences were meaningful to them, and many, I think, are quite remarkable. My hope in sharing these stories is that there will be more of an understanding that God truly works in many mysterious, wonderful, and unimaginable ways.

REMARKABLE SUPPORT

Several years ago, I met a lady who told me about how she slipped into a coma during the birth of her daughter, three years prior to our conversation. I had never met anyone who had been in a coma before, so I was curious if she had remembered anything while she was in that state of condition, and she replied, "I know that it may sound weird, but I talked to my guardian angel."

I was mesmerized, to say the least, and asked for more information. She told me that at that time, she had been going through a very trying relationship with her husband, and that she was under a lot of stress. She said that she sat inside a tunnel, with her sitting on one side of the tunnel and her guardian angel sitting across from her. She said that she never saw her guardian angel, but knew that it was so.

The angel told her that it was not her time to leave her earthly existence, and that she was supposed to stay and raise her daughter. The angel also told her to take her time and go back when she felt ready. The lady said that she sat in this tunnel and just poured her heart out to her guardian angel while the angel patiently listened to everything that was weighing her down.

Two weeks later, the lady woke up from the coma so that she could sort things out in her life as well as be a mom to her beautiful child.

REMARKABLE PEACE

Elizabeth was nineteen when she and her boyfriend, who later became her husband, were involved in a terrible motorcycle accident.

On this particular day, the young couple had been running errands and had just pulled out from a parking lot into the painted median in the middle of the road, where they were waiting for traffic to clear so that they could carry on to their next destination. While briefly resting, they were abruptly broadsided by a woman driving a Lincoln Navigator.

The driver of the SUV had crossed too early into the median in an effort to get into the left hand turn lane. She never noticed that the couple was sitting there on their motorcycle until she saw the boyfriend thrown into the air in front of her. Elizabeth was thrown into the air as well, was hit by another car, and landed hard on the pavement.

Elizabeth was coherent enough to take off her helmet because she was feeling claustrophobic with it on. At the same time, she sensed that there was something terribly wrong with her leg that got hit by the impact of the SUV. She heard her boyfriend moaning in horrible pain, so as Elizabeth started to attempt to pull her body toward the sound, she noticed a shadow come over her face.

A slightly overweight man with wavy blonde hair appeared within seconds. He knelt down and cupped Elizabeth's head between his hands. She felt an amazing peace overwhelm her senses, which kept her sane, as she tended to become hysterical pretty easily when something went wrong.

Elizabeth noticed a soft radiance surrounding this man's pleasant face, and he told her to lie still, and that everything was going to be okay. She asked him to keep talking to her, as she thought that by remaining focused on him that it would prevent her from realizing the chaos that was going on around her.

The man's soothing voice comforted her, and Elizabeth never noticed the transition between the kind man and the paramedics. She asked the paramedics about the man with the blonde hair because she wanted to thank him for being with her, and they replied that they never saw a man who matched her description.

To this day, Elizabeth believes that it was an angel who came to her rescue. It was if he was there, and then he was gone.

REMARKABLE VOICE

Distraught is how Ellie might describe herself. She was distraught because she had learned that afternoon that her only child had suffered a miscarriage. Ellie's daughter had been carrying twins after trying for years to conceive a child. She had finally done so, only to lose the much anticipated pregnancy. It was an extremely difficult day.

Later that night, shortly after she had fallen asleep, Ellie was jolted awake when she heard a young man's voice, clear as a bell, say into her right ear, "Don't worry. This time next year, you will be a grandmother." She bolted upright, wondering who was in her room, only to discover that no one was physically there, except her husband who was sound asleep next to her.

Ellie said that she will never forget the voice because it was the most beautiful voice she had ever heard, and it sounded as if the voice came from a young man around twenty years old. It was as if he had hovered over the bed to talk directly into her ear. She knew in her heart that it must have been her guardian angel and the message brought her such comfort and peace.

Ellie's daughter did wind up conceiving again, and this time, she was carrying triplets! There was a time during the pregnancy when the daughter had troubles and had to be admitted into the hospital, but Ellie felt at peace knowing that all would be well because of the angel's message to her.

A year after hearing the angel's comforting voice, Ellie and her husband were blessed with the birth of their grandchildren. She was so elated to finally have not just one, but three grandchildren to dote on.

REMARKABLE INSTRUCTION

Life had been pretty challenging for most of her twenty-three years, and late one Saturday night, Annette was at a point of desperation. Lying in bed and angrily voicing, "What do you want from me?" a loving, fatherly sounding voice clearly, yet firmly replied, "Go to a church upon the hill called High Pointe. Service starts at 9:30 Sunday morning. That is where I want you." Startled and a bit bewildered, she responded, "You want me to do what?" but got no reply.

Apprehensively, Annette got ready that next morning and drove to the little church at the top of a hill. She was uncomfortable because at that time, she worked in a motorcycle shop and mostly had jeans and black t-shirts in her closet, so she didn't feel like she would fit in. Annette arrived early, parked her car, and watched everyone file out of the church from the first service. She then got out of her car, and still feeling unsure on whether she should go into the church or not, Annette hid behind her car when she noticed the patrons beginning to file into the church for the next service. By the time everyone was inside, she voiced, "Okay, I came like you said, and now, I'm leaving."

Annette attempted to get into her car, but the door could not be opened. She went around to the passenger side and the door still could not be opened. There seemed to be a force that was keeping her from opening the doors to her car, and Annette realized that she just needed to give in. She said, "Really? You want me to go in there?"

Mustering up the courage, Annette walked into this little church and found a place to sit in the back row. An associate pastor shook her hand and she felt right at home. The band started to play inspirational music, and as she stood there with the rest of the congregation, an overwhelming peace and comfort enveloped her as tears flowed uncontrollably down her cheeks. Annette felt as though she was being physically supported because she really just wanted to collapse and release all of the heaviness that she had been carrying.

The next week, Annette was baptized and her life started to change for the better. She attended that little church for the next four years until she moved away.

REMARKABLE PROMPTING

A man was in the hospital battling a life-threatening, mysterious illness that had really stumped the doctors. The doctors had tried all of their tactics to no avail, but the man was now in a somewhat stable condition. The man's wife had been ever present at the hospital, never leaving her husband's side, until one day, a nurse suggested that she go home for the night to clean up and rest for a while. Exhausted, yet a bit uncertain if that would be the right move to make, she took the nurse's suggestion and decided to go home for a few hours.

While taking a few moments to take a shower, the lady suddenly felt an incredibly, intense feeling to hurry up and get back to the hospital. She knew that it was imperative that she be by her husband's side. Throwing herself together and then hurriedly getting into her car, the lady drove as quickly and safely as she could back to the hospital. Remarkably, there were no obstructions along the way, and there was even a parking space available that was close to the entrance when she arrived.

The lady went directly to her husband's hospital room, and the nurse noticed her and wondered out loud why she was back so soon. Within minutes after she arrived, her husband started to choke on blood that had filled up in his lungs. Immediately, she called for assistance, which led to prompt care, resulting in the rescue of her husband. It was very possible that her husband would not have survived had she not been by his side.

During the next few weeks, while the doctors were still trying to diagnose what was causing her husband to be so ill, the lady would take an occasional break and go outside for a while. There seemed to always be someone sitting on the park bench and the lady would become engaged in pleasant conversation. The conversation would lead to the same question and comment. The person would inquire who she was there for, and after telling her story, the person would respond, "Don't worry. He is going to be fine."

The questions and comments were so repetitive that at one point, her curiosity got the best of her that she hid behind a tree to see if someone was delivering this message to the person sitting on the bench. The lady felt foolish after a while as she never saw anyone approach the park bench, so she finally accepted that the message was divine and that it was meant to ease her concerns about her husband's state of health. She found this to be very comforting as she knew that all would be okay.

Sure enough, the problem was finally diagnosed as a rare virus that was unfamiliar to the doctors, as the man had contracted the illness in another region of the country while on a hunting trip. Now the doctors could properly treat the infection and the man was eventually well enough to go home.

REMARKABLE DIRECTION

My Uncle Patrick was very concerned one afternoon when he could not find his keys. Every key that was important to him hung on that key chain. He looked everywhere that he could think of and even had friends come over to help him search for the keys to no avail. After spending hours focused on the search, he gave up and went to bed.

Uncle Patrick woke up very early the next morning and my uncle, who was not a praying kind of man, said "God, please give me some light so I can find my keys." Then he got dressed for the day and ventured outside.

The sun was just coming up, and he noticed to the east that the sun was shining on a trash dumpster. He felt prompted to walk over to the dumpster, all the while thinking to himself that there was no way that his keys would be in the garbage.

He lifted the lid, and the sun filtered through the trees perfectly to where my uncle noticed something golden, glistening in the pile of trash. He had forgotten to put on his glasses, so he wasn't quite sure what he was reaching for but thought that he would give it a try, and he discovered that it was his set of keys! A gold key was perfectly reflecting the sun's rays so that it would grab his attention. He looks up to the sky and says, "Thanks, God, for the light."

My uncle was one happy, happy man!

REMARKABLE ASSURANCE

Storie runs a precious tea room and book store in Glen Rose, Texas, called The Storiebook Cafe. Storie had poured her heart and soul into creating a wonderful environment for her patrons in this small town. She didn't own her little shop, however, and the owners of the property were going through a messy divorce which put her business at stake. Storie was pretty worried about potentially losing what she had worked so hard for, so she was under a lot of stress.

One day, wonderful friends, who manage an antique shop near her business, brought by a piece of furniture that they had purchased at an auction. These friends love to pick up fun useful items for Storie to use in her tea room, and she usually treats them to a meal as they refuse to accept money for the items that they pick up for her.

Storie decided that she would put the dresser into the kitchen to use for storage and realized that it still had assorted items in the drawers. She stayed outside of her shop to empty the drawers into the trash can, while her friends moved the dresser to the kitchen. Then she returned to work, still carrying the weight of worry about what was going to happen to the business that she so loved.

Later that day, Storie went out to her car to leave for the evening, and perfectly placed on the pavement beside the driver's side door was a precious wooden angel pin. The angel was not much more than an inch tall and was wearing a tiny white cotton dress, as well as a sweet smile that seemed to be meant for Storie. It must have fallen out of one of the drawers when the dresser was moved, but it was as if it had been placed precisely for her to see.

Storie was lifted and knew that it was a sign that everything was going to be okay, which it was, because everything worked out for her to continue pouring love into the business that was dear to her heart.

REMARKABLE ESCORT

Jill worked for a consulting firm and would fly weekly from Minneapolis to Los Angeles for business. She always stayed at the same hotel when in Los Angeles, and on this particular morning, she needed to catch a 6:40 flight to fly home, but she wound up oversleeping and woke up with a start at 6:00.

Stressed and determined to try to make her flight, Jill bolted out of bed and threw herself together. She gathered her belongings, tossed the keys to the hotel clerk, and jumped into the rental car.

Jill was driving as fast as she felt comfortable driving, when all of a sudden, a white car passed her by and pulled right in front of her car. The white car was breaking the speed limit, and she sensed that she should just stay right behind that car and drive the same speed. She was only ten miles from the Ontario airport, but knew that she had just minutes to be able to make the flight back to Minneapolis. The white car put on its blinker to indicate that it was exiting the exact exit that she needed to take, so she did the same.

The exit ramp led down a hill and at the bottom of the hill was a stop sign, and at this intersection, you could either turn to the right or to the left. Jill took the exit, she looked away briefly to check the time, then she looked back up to focus on the road ahead, and the white car was nowhere within sight! Once she was on the road that would lead to the airport, Jill looked in her rearview mirror and confirmed that the car was, indeed, nonexistent.

Thankfully, Jill made the flight with not a second to spare, and the more that she thought about the curious way that she seemed to be escorted that morning, the more she believed that it must have been an angel that had assisted her in getting to the airport just in the nick of time.

REMARKABLE INTERVENTION

Back in her college years, Patti and her roommate were driving on a highway, headed for the Texas coast for a girlfriend's wedding. They were halfway to their destination and were enjoying listening to music while deep in conversation when a car, with college-age guys, pulled up to the left of their car and began flirting with the girls.

The guys were having fun and would increase their speed anytime Patti drove faster and would decrease their speed anytime Patti slowed down. They were doing their best to get the girls' attention, but the girls had an agenda so they would not allow themselves to become engaged in the horseplay. So they kept up their conversation with each other and stayed focused on making it to the coast. After a minute or so, the guys gave up, and drove ahead of the girls.

Patti was driving fast, yet was following a little too close to the guys in front, and after briefly taking her attention off the road to change a cassette tape, she looked up and realized that the car ahead had come to a complete stop. Patti gasped and immediately slammed on her brakes with the knowing that there was not enough time to stop her car without ramming into the back of the car in front of her.

The sound of screeching tires is all that Patti remembers before coming to the realization that her car was now perfectly resting to the right of the car they had been previously following. Somehow, Patti's car wound up on the shoulder of the road instead of in the middle of what could have been a tragic scenario.

Dazed and trying to wrap her head around what had just happened, Patti looked to her left and locked eyes with the guys who looked just as stunned and perplexed, while her roommate was shouting, "Oh my God! That was some great driving!"

A train was now barreling down the tracks in front of the two cars, and remarkably, the girls and guys were able to safely carry on to their next destination, a bit rattled, yet thankfully, intact.

There were lives still to live.

REMARKABLE SAVE

The baseball game was over, and Teresa and her family headed out of the ball park towards the parking lot. It was a beautiful spring day, and the family was involved in casual conversation as they strolled along the sidewalk that led in the direction of their cars.

Teresa was aware that her five-year-old son, Drew, had ventured a little too far ahead of them. She was about to call his name to have him come back toward her, when he picked up speed to run into the parking lot, and much to their horror, right in front of a Suburban that had no chance of stopping before it hit Drew.

Everything happened so fast, and from the angle that they had on Drew, Teresa and her mother and brother noticed the striped shirt that he was wearing was billowed out and that the small boy was curiously elevated above the hood of the truck. The driver of the Suburban did not slow down, so had apparently never even noticed the terrifying situation at hand.

Teresa and her family caught up to Drew who was standing peacefully, on a grassy median, smiling at them. A mixture of emotions ran through the adults while they made sure that Drew was not harmed in any way. After determining that all was well and after collecting their senses, the family parted ways and went home.

Later that evening, when Teresa had her kids in the bathtub, she calmly asked Drew what had possessed him to bolt across a lane meant for traffic, when he knew that he should always have an adult by his side when crossing a street.

Drew, who was calm and composed, said that he saw his Paw Paw, and so he ran to see him so that he could say bye to him. Paw Paw was Teresa's father-in-law, who had just passed away the week prior to the incident.

Drew said, "Paw Paw lifted me in his arms when I ran to see him!"

REMARKABLE LIGHT

Kathy attended Bible study classes that were led by a lady named Maria. One day, Maria asked Kathy and another class member to join her to pray for her friend's father, who had been released from a hospital after a lengthy stay and was now in hospice care in his home.

Kathy, a woman of great faith in the power of God, eagerly accepted the invitation to join Maria. After arriving at the man's home, they gathered around his hospital bed along with his family. The man, who had once been a strong, vibrant man, was now emaciated and decrepit and appeared to be twenty years older than his sixty plus years of age.

Maria began to pray in Spanish, and immediately, the man seemed to become agitated. His arms and feet began to move as if he was uncomfortable. The more that Maria prayed, the more agitated the man became. The man's family was so surprised because he had been unable to move or to speak for quite some time.

At one point, the ladies joined Maria in saying, "Is Jesus Christ your Lord and Savior?", repeating the question a few times more. By this time, the man was thrashing his arms and legs. Suddenly, the man opened his eyes, and while appearing stunned yet smiling at the same time, reached his hands toward the ceiling and shouted something in Spanish.

Enthralled and a bit confused because Kathy did not understand the language, she asked Maria what the man had voiced and Maria replied, "He said, 'The light…the light…who turned on the light?'"

Kathy and the ladies happily joined the family in rejoicing in the glory of the moment, and the man lived several more weeks before he peacefully passed away.

REMARKABLE PROTECTION

Max loved school, and on this particular January morning in 1965, she woke up not feeling very well. Her mother decided that she would need to stay home for the day, so when the lady who drove the van that picked up parochial school kids in Albuquerque stopped by for Max, her mother informed the driver that Max would not be attending school that day and waved her onward.

A short while later, after watching her two younger sisters get dressed and ready for the day, Max was feeling better. She really wanted to go to school, so she begged her mother to please let her go and asked her to drop her off in front of the school, to which her mother consented as she agreed that Max was not ill after all.

Max put on her school uniform, stockings, socks over her stockings, and oxford shoes, then she grabbed her coat, hat, and satchel. Her mother took her to school and she had an enjoyable day until the nun, who became upset with a boy in the class, decided to hold the class a few minutes longer before letting them go for the day. Max was nervous because she knew that time was running out for catching the van that would take her home.

As soon as she made it out of the front doors of the elementary school, Max saw the van drive away. It was obvious that the driver was not aware that she needed to wait for her. Max knew that the next stop for the van would be the high school building, so she ran across the giant courtyard and through the high school only to miss the van that would take her home. She went back to the elementary school, and by this time, the nuns were hustling the kids out of the building, and after an attempt to get the nun's attention to no avail, the six-year-old rule follower left the building.

Max sat on the steps in front of the school watching parents pick their children up, and once they were all gone, she stood up and made the decision to walk home. She knew the route because she had months of experience paying attention to landmarks while looking out of the windows of the van. She was focused and intent on getting home, and she did not have an ounce of worry about making the trek. The trek, however, was an eighteen-mile trek, though Max was unaware of the scale of the task at hand.

Max felt sure that she could handle this venture as she knew that she had a guardian angel with her and she knew that she would be protected. Max knew this because she had been taught to believe in the assistance of guardian angels, and she pictured in her mind the framed picture that hung in her bedroom of a guardian angel guiding a young girl and boy across a rickety bridge. This comforted her and filled her with confidence and a knowing that she would be fine.

For hours, Max happily walked fast and, at times, skipped along streets and sidewalks being careful to stay safely away from the edge of the roads that would take her home. At one point, she needed to cross a four-lane street that had a median in the middle and she noticed an old man slowly walking toward her. He met up with her, no words were exchanged, and Max just knows that she needs to pay close attention to the man's feet and to follow exactly what he did.

Side by side, they stepped off the curb, crossed two lanes, and stepped up onto the median. They rested for a moment and then crossed two more lanes before stepping up onto the curb on the opposite side of the street. All the while, Max had been paying close attention to the man's shoes, and after breathing a deep sigh of relief, she happily looked up at the man and the man is not there anymore. Undaunted, Max carried on, finally mastering the Rio Grande Bridge, which was her only concern, and was now on the road that was a straight shot to her neighborhood. With miles to go, she happily hurried on.

Her hands were cold, as she had forgotten her gloves that morning, her arms were a little tired from carrying her satchel, and she was feeling a little hungry, but aside from that, Max remained focused and happy. She picked up speed when she finally made it to the fence line of the pasture that was close to home, and she, along with the horses on the other side of the fence, ran toward her neighborhood.

It was 8:45 by the time Max arrived on the front porch of her home and into the arms of an elated uncle and a mother who had been so very distraught with worry. By this time, Max had been missing for over six hours and family, friends, and police officers had been searching everywhere. Her classmates and their families had gone to mass to pray for her safe return and the news stations had broadcasted the story of a missing school girl.

Her mother could not understand why Max didn't use the dime that she always put in her sock in case Max needed to call home and her six-year-old self replied "You gave me two nickels!" After that, they made sure that Max had a much better understanding of money.

Almost fifty years has gone by since that remarkable experience and Max wonders how she would have made it safely across a major interchange, which she would have had to do in order to get home, and she doesn't remember doing that at all. She also did not realize that it was dark outside for a few hours before she arrived on her front porch and noticed that the porch light was on.

Under the protective wing of her guardian angel, Max was kept safe and out of harm's way.

REMARKABLE VISIT

The warmth of her mother's hand, sliding across her left palm and then interlocking fingers in a way that only a daughter would recognize, is what woke Elaine out of her sleep. For months now, Elaine had been depressed over the death of her beloved mother. She had spent a lot of her time curled up in the bed that was in her own home, that her mother had passed away in, trying desperately to hold on to the memories of her mother and praying that she would come back to her.

A couple of days after her mother's death, her mother had paid a visit to Elaine's husband during the night. She was as real as if she had never passed away. She told him that she was fine, but to please have people pray for her because she was in a state of transition and she needed more prayers because she wanted to go to heaven. She had asked him to please tell Elaine to let her go, which Elaine had an extremely hard time doing as her mother was only fifty-one years old when she had passed away.

Elaine prayed more than she had ever prayed in her life, and she slept a lot of the time with the hope that her mother would visit her like she had visited her husband months before. Now, Elaine is holding hands with the woman who had brought her such joy in life and who was now bringing her such immeasurable joy to the point that her heart is ready to explode! Elaine says to her mother, "You didn't die!" to which her mother replies, "Yes, I did."

Elaine feels weightless and so amazingly wonderful as she is sitting there, holding hands with her mother. Few words were exchanged as they smile at each other and the intensely bright yet not blinding light envelopes Elaine and the room. Elaine notices that her mother is standing in front of two enormous golden wooden doors with a wondrous light being emitted around the perimeters of the closed doors. Elaine just knows, without a doubt, that it is God that is behind the giant doors, and she is enamored at the purity of the light and everything feels just so right.

Elaine says to her mother, "I thought that you were in purgatory." And her mother replies, "Everybody's prayers helped." Elaine's mother looks so very healthy and happy and her mother, who is bursting with joy, says, "I made it! I am going to the Lord!" She says, "I will always be with you," and with that, she backs toward the doors as they are slowly sliding open, she turns her head and smiles at Elaine, then the doors slowly come to a close behind her.

The room is now dark as it is four o'clock in the morning, and Elaine is filled with such a sense of inexplicable happiness. Her heart, which had been so heavy with darkness for several months, was now so full of love! Elaine now knew that it was time to move on knowing that all was so very well with her mother, but first, it was time to call her sisters with the great news.

REMARKABLE INFORMATION

Morgan was concerned about his oldest daughter. It was 1983, and Kim had been home from college twice now for the holidays and during each occasion, while in the middle of conversation with her family, Kim's jaw locked up. This was very disconcerting for Kim as well as for her family as they had never had this experience before.

After the second incident, Morgan and his wife immediately took Kim to a reputable hospital to see if they could get help. The hospital wound up admitting Kim, and after two days of testing, sent her home with a prescription for a muscle relaxer, as they could not come up with an answer to the problem.

Dana, the younger of the two daughters, was eating lunch in the cafeteria at her college one day, when a girl with fair skin and golden brown hair came up and asked if she could join her. At first, she was a little surprised as there were plenty of other empty tables available, but she was happy to have the company. Dana learned that this girl was in one of her classes, which she was sure that she had never seen her in her class before, but she accepted what the girl told her.

They were having a pleasant conversation, when the topic came up about Dana's sister having problems that doctors could not diagnose. The girl said that she knew exactly what the problem was and told Dana that it was called temporomandibular joint (TMJ) disorder.

Dana jotted down the information along with the girl's name before they parted ways. Then she called her parents with the news that could possibly be helpful to Kim.

Eager to visit further with the young lady, Morgan called the college and mentioned that he would like to contact the girl who provided their daughter with such valuable information. The receptionist put Morgan on hold and came back saying that they did not have anyone registered in their school by the name that he provided them.

A visit to a family dentist confirmed that TMJ was the exact diagnosis, which was a new discovery at the time. This subsequently, led to the proper help for Kim.

Dana never again saw the girl who had joined her at lunch, and to this day, the family believes that an angel came forward with the information that they so desperately needed.

REMARKABLE ANSWER

Colleen sat in her car, wondering if she should venture into the gift shop. It was raining and she really did not have extra money to spend, yet she needed something that would help to reduce the stress that she had been under lately, and just being in that store would be comforting to her. Colleen knew that it would be helpful to spend some time browsing around.

Two of Colleen's three kids were now enrolled in a private elementary school because the public schools that her family was zoned to were falling way below state standards. She was now faced with the decision to homeschool her children. The cost of private school was so expensive and she and her husband wanted to save money for their kids' college funds.

Colleen knew that once she committed herself to homeschooling her children, that time to accomplish her tasks as a stay-at-home mom, or take on a part-time job, or just have a moment to herself, would be scarce. She was not sure if she had it in her to go this route. Colleen was under a lot of stress and worry and all that goes with it, so life was feeling pretty heavy.

Somewhat reluctantly, Colleen decided to venture out into the pouring rain and go into the gift shop. A woman, who sat behind the counter, somberly greeted her. After making a couple of rounds through the small shop, she picked up a few inexpensive candles and headed toward the counter. She really did not want to leave without buying a little something to support this small business.

Colleen mentioned to the woman how she thought that it would be fun to work in a shop like this, and the woman replied, "It gets me out of bed in the morning." While Colleen was curious about the odd response to her comment, the woman continued by saying, "I'm sorry. I don't mean to be a downer, but I just lost my nine-year-old son."

The woman carried on with her story and told Colleen how her son had joined a friend on an excursion to a lake that summer. He arrived home all safe and sound a few days later, seeming to be in fine condition. The boy woke up the next morning congested and having a headache as well as muscle aches and the woman took her son to the pediatrician, only to be sent away with a common diagnosis of the boy having a virus. Another day passed and the boy seemed to become more lethargic.

It was early the following morning when the woman and her husband woke up and were surprised to see their son standing in their bedroom all dressed and ready for the day. The father says, "Hey, buddy. Where are you going all dressed up?" and the boy replied, "The angels are coming for me. I've got to go now."

Terrified, the parents immediately rushed their son to the emergency room, only to tragically lose him later that afternoon from what wound up being an amoeba infection that he had contracted at the lake a few days prior.

Colleen left the shop with such a heavy sadness for the woman's loss, and she cried all of the way home. She knew that she was supposed to hear that heart-wrenching story because, as it turns out, the woman's son's name was the name of Colleen's oldest child, who just happened to be closing in on the age of nine.

Colleen cast all worries and concerns to the side and made the decision to homeschool her children and she never looked back. The kids have now all since graduated and have gone off to college.

I have mentioned a few times how things seem to flow and fall into balance when I just ask for the divine plan to be fulfilled in whatever is going on for that particular day. Here are just a few examples of what some may call coincidences, yet I believe that God and guardian angels have a hand in these very neat experiences that happen to people all of the time.

REMARKABLE TIMING

Wade and I had some friends, who we had not seen in a few years, come to town. We were really looking forward to spending time with this family, so we met downtown for lunch with plans to attend a baseball game afterwards. While at the restaurant, we discovered that they offered a shuttle service to the stadium, so we decided to take them up on the convenient ride. There were a total of seven of us and room for two more, so two ladies joined us for the trip to the ball park.

The shuttle driver said that she made repeated drives back and forth to drop off and pick up passengers, so she showed us where we should meet her after the game. We arrived at the stadium, said good-bye to the ladies, and parted ways. We watched a great game with our friends and then left for the shuttle. There were several thousand people who attended the game, so it took a while to file out of the ball park. We were up on the third level of the stadium, so we took the outdoor concrete ramp that zigzagged to the lower level.

As we stepped off the ramp, we came face-to-face with the two ladies, who rode the shuttle with us. They had just exited the stadium on the ground level, and not one person had crossed our paths before our paths met. Not one thing intercepted this chance encounter.

One of the ladies remarked, "Oh my God. What just happened? This is crazy!" I was thinking the same thing because there was no way that I could have arranged such a precise orchestration of the merging of two random paths.

This remarkable timing was certainly divine.

REMARKABLE REMINDER

I took Luke to San Antonio for a Texas history assignment in the spring of 2012. His job was to visit at least ten different historical sites, learn something interesting, and take pictures as well. Before we left on the trip, I grabbed a stack of *Angels Are God's Helpers* to donate to a children's hospital or an assistance ministry while we were in San Antonio. I failed to make time to research where I might drop these books off while we toured the city, so we left home without having an address or a name of a place to leave the books.

Luke and I spent a few hours one morning visiting the Alamo and other historical sites. We decided to drive out to see the Spanish missions, but before we left, I wanted to take him to see one more historical site while we were downtown. By this time, he was tired and really did not want to stop anywhere else, so I told him that we would only stop if we could find a parking space near the site.

Parking spaces were few and far between, so I thought that our chances of finding one might be slim. We arrived at the park, which took up a city block and was surrounded by parallel parking spaces. There was no place to park my car on the street that we were on, so I took a right and still there were no spaces available. We rounded the next corner and I saw a perfect parking space for my small car, so I squeezed my car into the tight spot.

To my amazement, directly across the street from the parking space was an enormous eight story tile mosaic of a guardian angel with a young boy. It was a children's hospital! I was led right to it when it was not even on my mind to do so. My car sat right across from an entrance to the hospital, so it is needless for me to say, that I went inside to donate the stack of books that I had brought on the trip with me.

I was so thankful for God's divine guidance that led me here and confirmed for me that my heart is in the right place regarding the distribution of that precious gift from God.

REMARKABLE ADVICE

After noticing the repeated questions that got me to this point of writing this book, I now pay attention to words that are presented to me through other people. Last summer, I drove Sue, my wonderful mom-in-law, and Luke to the beach for the weekend in Sue's SUV.

The morning after our arrival, we went to the grocery store to pick up a few items for our stay. After shopping, we loaded Sue's vehicle, then prepared to leave. I put the key into the ignition and the engine barely started and then would immediately die. I made several attempts to start her SUV before I got out of the truck to see if I could find someone to help us out. It was so strange because everything had been just fine with the SUV not thirty minutes before and it showed no signs of there being any problems.

There was a man who was getting into his car next to ours, so I asked him if he knew anything about cars. He said that he did and he tried starting the truck a few times and assessed that we probably had a clogged fuel filter. It was a Sunday and we were not anywhere close to a decent-sized town that could provide some options, so I thought that it might be impossible to find a mechanic. I went inside the grocery store to see if they sold fuel filters. I knew that it was a long shot, but I thought that I would try.

I approached the man who was behind the customer service counter, mentioned the problem that I was having, and he asked me if there were grocery cards with barcodes attached to the key chain. I said that as a matter of fact, there were three attached to the keys. He said that he was just listening to a favorite mechanic on the radio the day before, and a caller had called in with this exact problem.

The man told me to take the cards off the key chain. Then he said to put the key into the keyhole in the drivers' side door and turn it to the right and then turn it to the left, which apparently talks to the car's computer. Then the man said to try to start the car.

I thanked him for the information, did what he advised me to do, and the truck started and stayed on! I drove us back to the house, and I called the man at the store to thank him for his help and to tell him that the information he provided me worked out after all.

He replied that it must be a "God thing," because of the timing of the whole situation, and I smiled and thought to myself, "It's a 'God thing' all right. It is a 'God thing.'"

REMARKABLE MANIFESTATION

It was the month of February, and I was helping to set tables for women's night at our church. The job that I was assigned was to place enough paper sacks, stickers, markers, and such in the center of each table, so the ladies could decorate sacks for Valentine's Day.

The problem that I noticed immediately was that there might not be enough stickers to distribute for the thirty tables that would each seat eight ladies. I diligently set aside thirty stacks of eight paper sacks and then carefully trimmed and distributed various stickers and set them on top of the sacks. By this time, another lady had joined me, and we each double and triple counted what we had because we were really stretching the amount of stickers to make it work out fairly well.

We began placing the sets of items in the middle of the tables, and by the time we had finished our assignment, the lady who was organizing the event said that we would need enough for two more tables. I thought, *This is going to really limit the amount of stickers the ladies have to choose from.* I was now going to start pulling stickers off the tables to try to make enough for two more tables.

At that moment, I turned back toward the table where we had been initially working, and sitting on top of the table were two piles of stickers! I was dumfounded, to say the least. I recounted the tables confirming that there were indeed thirty set tables, and I said to the lady who had helped me out, "You are my witness. There were thirty stacks of stickers, right?" She replied "Yes…there were thirty stacks of stickers."

Now there were thirty-two.

REMARKABLE CALCULATION

I was packaging up a stack of thirty copies of *Angels Are God's Helpers* to mail to a children's hospital. I had recently found the perfect size box for the books to fit inside, and Wade had recommended that I tie a ribbon around the books before I put them into the box for shipment. I shopped around and found bolts of ribbon that would match the front cover of the book. Each bolt held seven yards of ribbon (252 inches).

I played around with the ribbon, trying to get an idea of how much it might take to make a cross formation around the stack of books, winding up with a nice size bow on top—not too big and definitely not too small. I did not want to waste ribbon, so it took a little while for me to be confident enough to cut it, which I did, and was pleasantly surprised that it made a perfect size bow on top.

I took the ribbon off of the stack of books so that I could measure it and record the size for future packages. It measured 63 inches. I then decided to calculate how many ribbons I would get off of one bolt, so I picked up a pencil and thought that I would challenge my brain the old-fashioned way. I deducted 63 from

252 and came up with 189. I then subtracted another 63 which left 126, while subtracting another 63 coming up with 63.

Incredibly, there was no excess ribbon that would go to waste!

REMARKABLE LIFT

There was a morning in early 2010 when I had asked God for something to lift the spirits of my son who was heavy with sadness. It had been a difficult week for our family, as we had just said good-bye to our beloved Labrador retriever a few days prior. Sammi was the best and most amazing dog that I had ever been around, and she graced our family for six short years. We were so blessed to know her and to share a segment of our life with her.

Luke attended private school for his middle school years, and to get to this school, we had to maneuver along two lane back country roads. That morning, after about ten silent minutes into our twenty-minute trek, Luke all of a sudden starts to shout, "Mom, Look! That's a bald eagle! That's a bald eagle!" This was something that I had never seen, as of that time, in all of the days that I had lived in Texas.

The sight of this majestic symbol of freedom could not have been more perfectly timed nor orchestrated. Just as we had reached the straight shot, after traveling along many bends in the road before we reached the next bend, a bald eagle, that was being chased by a flock of crows, flew toward our car from the opposite end. Our paths met precisely in the middle of this stretch of road, and the eagle flew over our car as if it had always been a part of a well thought-out and executed plan.

Luke was lifted, which lifted me, and all that I did was ask—and that made me so very happy!

REFLECTIONS OF A REMARKABLE JOURNEY

January 14, 2014, was when it all came together. That was the day that I let myself print out the final copy of *Remarkable Guidance*, and it felt right. It had been close to two years since I started this journey of following through with this desire to write this book, and it has been a wonderful and joyous experience for me because I honestly did not know that I had it in me to do this. It's cliché, but it is the truth.

There is such a power in the silence, and this is where much of the guidance took place. The original thoughts that were coming to me—"Just write. It will all come together," was exactly what happened! I stayed true to the inner guidance and the promptings that I felt to keep applying myself to this desire and to keep ignoring the several years of dust that has been accumulating on the baseboards in my home. That project will have my attention soon enough as it is, but I still have priorities that are more important than dust that seems never ending.

I learned so much more about God and life as I wrote, so I kept writing, and sometimes, information would just pour out and I would think, *Where did that come from*? Or I would wake up with songs in my head, and when I finally cued in to the lyrics that had been repeating themselves over and over, there was usually an inspiring message to keep doing what I was doing. Many times, God or Jesus or angels were a part of the lyrics. I listen to all types of music so the songs weren't always a Christian song, but the words always had a message that caused me to smile.

These confirmative ways kept me focused on following through with my dream. I think that God and the angels have many techniques of reminding us that we are not alone and I think that they are in ways that are meaningful, especially if a positive feeling is generated from within. Most, I believe, go unnoticed.

Discovering a ladybug on my car door as I am about to get into my car, when there does not seem to be a flower or a tree anywhere in my line of sight, always causes me to smile. Or when I find a coin on the ground with the meaningful words "In God We Trust" embossed on it, it fills my heart with appreciation. When I notice repetitive numbers or letters or ones that are in a sequential order, which I always interpret as things are synchronized and are flowing and are in a perfect order, I am always inspired. Everything that lifts my spirit keeps me focused on God and keeps me true to the desires of my heart.

I completed the healing process of some remnants that were still a part of my suitcase of issues, and interestingly enough, I would look at that old worn-out garment and wonder, "Why did I hold on to you for so long? Why was I so afraid of you? You aren't as bad as I thought you were," which leads me to believe that God gives us only what we can handle in increments of time. So what used to be a big deal to me was not such a big deal after I had walked a few paths and became conditioned and strengthened in many ways.

My family and a handful of friends who knew that writing this book was a passion of mine would inquire at times how close I was to completing it. I would always say "I know that I will know it when I know it!" because just when I thought that I was close to completing this book, I would wake up with ideas of more information that I should find a place for or something that I should rephrase or delete or move to another chapter. When the ideas stopped coming to me, I knew that I was close to completion.

The molding and transforming of this book has been an incredible process, and it reminds me of the molding and transforming of me. It's all an opportunity to learn and in the end it is all about growth and mastery. This book is better than it was when I first printed it out over a year ago, and God knows that I am better than I was when I first started to crawl, then toddle, then maneuver along on the path of life.

I will end this book with an extraordinary dream that I had several months ago. It kind of sums up this remarkable journey that I have been on.

I was on a trek. I noticed that I was wearing a comfortable shirt, shorts, and hiking boots, and I had on my back a perfectly weighted backpack—not too light and not too heavy—and I wasn't in a hurry. I was just on a purposeful mission to move forward.

I was in a wooded environment, and it was an absolutely beautiful day with the sun filtering through the tall pine trees. The path that I was on was wide and was covered in pine needles and there were other people on this path as well who were going in the same direction. No one was talking, and in fact, they all seemed to be on an independent journey. The sounds of nature, which are so pleasing to the senses, created a peaceful, happy feeling all around.

I observed that there was a gently flowing river that needed to be crossed that was about thirty feet wide. I was on the right side of this body of water, and I saw other people swimming across it to get to the other side where there were many more people walking across a sun-drenched meadow and up and over a distant hill.

I knew that I needed to cross that river, so without a concern, I jumped into the water so that I could swim to the other side. My body pierced the water, but what was strange was that I did not resurface. I kept going down. I had a sense that there was no floor to this body of water.

I wasn't frightened at all because just as I was about to become concerned about the situation that I was in, a force rescued me and rocketed me out from underneath approximately twelve feet of water. We travelled all the way to the tops of the pine trees where we stopped and hovered for a few seconds, all the while enjoying the most incredible feeling of weightlessness.

This phenomenal dream seemed to be a very real experience and one that gave me some insight into a battle between light and dark. I can't imagine and don't really want to imagine what might be going on behind the veil, the light forces rising up against the dark forces. I can't imagine what they must face, but what I can imagine is the love for God that the light forces must have to want to help bring forth more light across a troubled world.

That I can see.

What I can't see is living life without the assistance of the forces of light, my guardian angels, who are here to guide and assist me in many remarkable ways, as I continue on my trek through the sun-drenched meadow toward and eventually up and over the distant hill.

A place that is beyond my comprehension, where there must be an even clearer understanding of God.